teen's

guides

LIVING
with
SKIN
CONDITIONS

Also in the
Teen's Guides series

teen's
guides

LIVING
with
SKIN
CONDITIONS

Sarah L. Chamlin, M.D.
with E. A. Tremblay

☑️Checkmark Books®
An imprint of Infobase Publishing

Living with Skin Conditions

Checkmark Books
An imprint of Infobase Publishing, Inc.
132 West 31st Street
New York, NY 10001

Library of Congress Cataloging-in-Publication Data

Chamlin, Sarah L.
 Living with skin conditions / by Sarah L. Chamlin, with E. A. Tremblay.
  p. cm. — (Teen's guides)
 Includes bibliographical references and index.
 ISBN-13: 978-0-8160-7911-7 (hardcover : alk. paper)
 ISBN-10: 0-8160-7911-0 (hardcover : alk. paper)
 ISBN-13: 978-0-8160-7912-4 (pbk. : alk. paper)
 ISBN-10: 0-8160-7912-9 (pbk. : alk. paper) 1. Skin—Care and hygiene.
2. Skin—Diseases. I. Tremblay, E. A. II. Title.
 RL87.C43 2010
 616.5—dc22   2009025496

Checkmark Books are available at special discounts when purchased in bulk quantities for businesses, associations, institutions or sales promotions. Please call our Special Sales Department in New York at (212) 967-8800 or (800) 322-8755.

You can find Facts On File on the World Wide Web at http://www.factsonfile.com

Text design by Annie O'Donnell
Composition by Hermitage Publishing Services
Cover printed by Art Print, Taylor, Pa.
Book printed and bound by Maple-Vail Book Manufacturing Group, York, Pa.
Date printed: April, 2010
Printed in the United States of America

10 9 8 7 6 5 4 3 2 1

This book is printed on acid-free paper.

CONTENTS

You and the Skin You're In

Have you ever had one of those days? The kind of day when you can't find your iPOD; you're running late for school, your mom is nagging you to eat breakfast, and to top it all off, a huge red pimple that appeared in the middle of the night is sitting right in the center of your forehead? Of course, you can survive a few hours without listening to your latest downloads, calm your mother down by grabbing an apple, and bring a note to the school office for being late. But you really could have done without the unwanted visitor on your face. What's up with that, anyway? In fact, what's up with your skin in general? Why won't it behave?

WHAT YOU'RE ALL WRAPPED UP IN

Skin is more than simply the packaging you came in. It's an organ, just like your lungs, heart, and brain. All organs have a few things in common. All organs are made of different kinds of tissue. The skin has three kinds of tissue: epithelial (the lining), connective, and nerve. Every organ type is differentiated, which means it has its own unique shape and structure. Also, organs are specialized, which means they have their own particular jobs to do to help keep you alive and healthy. Finally, every organ is part of a system. Systems are families in which two or more organs work together toward a common goal. For example, your brain and nerves belong to your nervous system; your stomach, intestines, and several others to the digestive system; and your heart and blood vessels to the circulatory system. So what about the skin?

YOUR BUILT-IN SECURITY SYSTEM

Your skin is the largest organ in the *integumentary system,* which also includes your hair, fingernails, toenails, tooth enamel, oil glands, and sweat glands. All of these work together to keep everything inside of you safe, snug, and warm and to warn you when anything threatens that inner security. Here is how your skin contributes.

It keeps your temperature steady. Your body can overheat for many reasons, including exercise, a warm environment, or *infection.* Your skin cools things off by sweating, which moves the heat out, and evaporation, which sends the moisture into the air. On the other hand, if you start to get too cold, your skin helps hold the heat inside of you and keeps itself warm by circulating more blood close to its surface.

It protects you. It's important to keep the world outside of you separate from the one inside of you, and that's exactly the service your skin provides. It acts as a protective covering that keeps all of your other organ systems safe from germs, dirt, chemicals, sunlight, and everything else in the environment that can be harmful.

It allows you to feel things. The nerve endings in your skin allow you to feel texture, pressure, heat, cold, and pain. Of course, it would be nice to skip the pain part, but that's one important way your body has of warning you that you're in danger. If something is burning your skin, for example, you need to know this immediately, so that you can move away from the heat.

It gets rid of what you don't need. Sweating does more than move heat out of your body. It can get rid of excess salt, chemicals, and toxins that you're better off without.

It alerts your immune system. When anything manages to get past your skin barrier—such as germs that enter through a cut or other wound—little messengers called *Langerhans cells* attach to the invader and send signals to your immune system that say, "Come and get this guy!" These invaders, also called *antigens,* are troublemakers, and the immune system does its best to get rid of them quickly.

Skin Facts: Did You Know?

The skin is the largest organ in your body. A full-grown adult's skin can weigh as much as six pounds and contain 10 percent of the body's blood supply.

It makes vitamin D. One way people get vitamin D, which helps you absorb calcium from your food, is through sunlight. Sunlight contains ultraviolet rays, which activate a form of vitamin D, called D3, in blood that passes close to the surface of your skin.

IT'S NOT AS SIMPLE AS YOU MIGHT THINK

Although your skin looks like a single sheet of material that covers you all over, it actually has a pretty amazing and complex structure. First of all, everyone has two types of skin—thin and hairy, and thick and hairless. The second type covers parts of your body that are often in contact with other surfaces, such as the palms of your hands and the soles of your feet. You don't want hair growing in those places, as they're tough and thick and generally exposed to a lot of rubbing and friction. Everywhere else, you're covered by the first type. On average, your skin is two millimeters thick—about as thick as a penny—but its thickness varies by location.

Regardless of type, your skin comes in layers. The protective top layer is the *epidermis.* It contains cells called melanocytes that give skin its color. The epidermis is constantly manufacturing fresh new cells, which, over a period of two to four weeks, make their way to the surface. A skin cell, however, has a brief life span. It will die just before it reaches the surface—which means that the skin you can see is really a thin layer of dead cells.

The second layer, the *dermis,* contains sensory nerves, *sebaceous* (oil) glands, sweat glands, and lots of blood vessels. It also contains two proteins, *collagen* and *elastin,* which keep your skin smooth, plump, and flexible. As you grow older, your supplies of collagen and elastin diminish. As a result, wrinkles form and your skin doesn't snap back into place as well after it's been stretched.

Skin Facts: Did You Know?

Your skin sheds up to 30,000 dead cells every minute. That's nearly nine pounds a year!

Under the dermis lies the subcutaneous layer, which is made mostly of fatty tissue. This layer helps keep your insides warm, acts as a shock absorber against bumps and blows, and connects your skin to the various tissues underneath, such as muscle. It's also where most of your hair roots, called follicles, are located.

UNSIGHTLY CHANGES

As you go through *puberty*—the transition from childhood to adulthood—your body is going through many changes. Your baby fat is disappearing and you are assuming a more mature shape. Many boys are becoming more muscular, while girls may develop curves. Hair is appearing in places other than your head, your voice is changing, and you're probably growing taller.

You're also changing in other ways. You're starting to think for yourself, gain more freedom in your social life, and feel some of the pressures of growing up with regard to future career, money, sex, and relationships.

With all of this going on, you may well be going through one of the most exciting times you will ever experience, but also one of the most nerve-racking. There is a good chance that you're feeling anxious about nearly everything in your life—school, relationships, the future, and not least of all, the way you look. And of course, this is exactly the moment when your skin has decided to go crazy.

Almost everyone has to deal with acne, whether it's mild or severe, at some point in his or her life. That probably seems like pretty unhelpful information. But because the condition is so common, we have a pretty good idea of what to expect from particular types of acne and have developed effective ways of treating and preventing it.

Acne is the result of hormonal changes that happen when you reach puberty. These changes can give you grief in other ways as well. For example, it can cause a girl to grow hair in places where she really does not want it, such as on her chin or over her upper lip. It can also cause either a boy or a girl to sweat excessively—a condition called hyperhidrosis.

There are also skin conditions unrelated to hormones that—while not as common as acne—can be just as upsetting and embarrassing. Some kids cope with *psoriasis* or *eczema,* which can make the skin look inflamed, scaly, and cracked. Others may develop an excessive number of *moles.* And some African-American teens have to live with a pigment disorder called vitiligo. Many of these conditions are related to genetics, which means they run in families.

During your teen years, you are also more likely to suffer skin injuries from sports and—let's face it—from taking more risks than either young kids or adults generally do. (You will rarely, for example, catch a grown-up or a five-year-old drag-racing, an activity that can land you in the hospital with burns, bruises, cuts, scrapes, and other crash-related injuries.) And then, of course, there is a whole world of infections—bacterial, fungal, and viral—that can be passed by any close personal contact, including sports and acts of intimacy.

SKIN CARE

Whether a skin condition is the result of hormonal changes, family history, infections, or injury, you don't have to throw your hands up and surrender to it. You can do a lot to help keep your skin healthy, clear, and attractive. Here's how.

Keep it clean. Although it is obviously smart to keep yourself clean, you don't want too much of a good thing. Over-scrubbing, taking long baths or showers, washing with very hot or cold water, or using harsh soap can deplete the skin of its natural moisturizers, causing unsightly irritation, dryness, and cracking. And by the way, scrubbing too much can actually make acne worse. Here are the four most important rules for cleansing:

1. **Use a mild soap.** Look for soap with a pH of 7. The pH of a substance tells you how acidic or alkaline (the opposite of acidic) it is. A 7 indicates "neutral," or a perfect balance between the two. Also, don't use bubble baths and scented soaps. They're harsh and irritating. Any bar or liquid soap that has a balanced pH and contains no fragrances will probably fit the bill. Your local drug store should have

plenty of choices, so read the labels and find a product that works for you.

2. **Use warm water.** Overly hot water can cause your skin to become very dry. Icy cold water, on the other hand, is no one's idea of a great sensation. Your best bet is lukewarm water.

3. **Set a time limit.** Taking a gentle, warm shower or bath can help to hydrate your skin, which will keep it moist and soft. Overdoing it, however, has the opposite effect. Lengthy contact with water soaks away your skin's natural protective oil, leaving your skin dry and maybe even flaky. Limit your bath or shower time to 10 minutes.

4. **Moisturize your body and face.** Because moisturizing creams and lotions help hold water in your skin, keeping it soft, supple, and healthy, it is always a good idea to apply some to your body at least once a day, preferably right after your bath or shower. However, not all moisturizers are created equal. There are some you might want to avoid, such as those made with fragrances, nut butters, or other foods. They can cause an allergic reaction in some people. Products that come in a tub or tube—creams—tend to be thicker and are often the best choice for very dry body skin. Vaseline and Aquaphor are the gold standard for this type of moisturizer, but they tend to be heavy and greasy. During the summer, you may want to use something lighter, so buy a lotion that dispenses through a pump. These products are thinner because they contain less oil. Most teens, of course, would rather not go through their day feeling greasy, so you might try taking your shower and applying a moisturizer at bedtime. Any product you use on your face should be oil-free and *non-comedogenic,* which means that it is unlikely to promote acne. There are plenty of great products to choose from, so don't settle for anything you don't like. If one doesn't please you, try another. And don't be fooled into thinking that high-priced department-store concoctions are best. They are no more effective than the less expensive products you can find at your local drugstore.

Avoid the sun. Although you might think that sunshine gives your skin a nice healthy glow, light rays—ultraviolet light—actually do a lot of damage. These rays can make you develop wrinkles before your time, leave your skin looking leathery, cause you to form more moles and unsightly brown spots, and, in the worst cases, give you skin can-

Skin Facts: Did You Know?

A SPF 15 sunscreen doesn't mean it's 15 times more powerful than one with an SPF of 1. It means it will keep you from burning 15 times *longer* than wearing no sunscreen at all.

cer. Just for good measure, this kind of light can damage your eyesight as well. You can't stay out of the sun completely, of course, but you can protect yourself. Wear a hat to protect your head and sunglasses to guard your eyes. Remember, a baseball hat only covers your forehead and eyes. A hat with a three-inch brim is better and will cover your face and neck. Most importantly, use a sunscreen or sunblock with a sun protection factor (SPF) of at least 15. Many moisturizers have sunscreen already added to them—something to consider when you're choosing one. Finally, a word about tanning booths. Some kids are under the impression that a few minutes under an ultraviolet lamp is safer than sitting out on the beach. In fact, the light you receive in a booth is just as dangerous as that from the sun because it's so intense, maybe even more so. The light you are exposed to in tanning booths can cause skin cancer, just like natural sunlight can.

Don't smoke. This is really a no-brainer. You already know that smoking causes lung cancer, ruins your circulation, and destroys your heart. It can also give you cancer of the mouth, bladder, pancreas, and others—11 cancers in all. Of course, all of these are consequences that could happen in the future and may not seem very relevant now. What is relevant now is that smoking gives you bad breath, discolors your teeth and fingers, makes your clothes and hair smell horrible, and can turn light-colored skin to a sallow yellow-gray. When you reach full adulthood, you may also begin to develop premature wrinkles. How? Tobacco smoke breaks down collagen in your skin—the protein that keeps it plump, smooth, and elastic. It also starves your skin cells of the oxygen they need. Cigarettes produce carbon monoxide—the same poisonous stuff that comes out of the exhaust pipe of a car. When you inhale this gas, it moves from your lungs into your bloodstream and takes the place of the normal, healthful oxygen that should be there instead. Your blood, in turn, delivers the carbon

---

Skin Facts: Did You Know?

You can start to see premature wrinkling and sagging on your face and other parts of your body, such as your inner arms, after smoking for only 10 years. So if you started lighting up when you were 12, you may begin to see the effects by the time you're 22.

---

monoxide to your skin—again, in place of oxygen. It's almost like suffocating your skin cells. By the way, cigarettes contain lots of other disgusting chemicals, including poisons such as arsenic, cyanide, and ammonia. To top it all off, smoking causes you to squint, forming lines at the corners of your eyes, and to purse your lips, creating deep wrinkles around your mouth.

Don't drink alcohol. Alcohol can affect your appearance in several ways. For one, it can make you gain weight. For another, it can dehydrate your body and dry out your skin. And because it causes your blood vessels to widen, it can also make you look red and blotchy. If you're underage, add to those risks the chance that you could be arrested—no one looks good in a mug shot.

BODY ART

Body art such as piercing and tattooing appears in nearly every culture around the world, including our own. The attractiveness and appropriateness of any ornamentation that affects your skin is, of course, a matter of taste, and whether or not you have any of these procedures done is a matter of very personal choice. But before deciding whether or not to insert a pin through your tongue, inject dye permanently into your skin, or even pierce your earlobes, there are some important issues to consider. These procedures have some risks, and if things go wrong, the price can be high.

Piercings. Remember, your skin is designed to keep in the good stuff, such as water, and shut out the bad stuff, such as *bacteria* and *fungus.* When you pierce it with a piece of metal, you're opening a doorway to all kinds of nasty intruders that would otherwise be turned away, including bloodborne diseases, germs, and fungi. If you use a needle that has already been used by someone with an infection such as hepatitis or HIV, you can inherit their infection. These can be very serious, even deadly.

Germs and fungi can cause swelling, redness, pain, foul odor, and pus—in other words, skin infections. In the worst cases—although these are very rare—they can spread to the bloodstream and cause serious illness or even death. Infections in cartilage, the semi-hard tissue that gives your ears their shape and separates the two sides of your nose, offer their own special problems. For one thing, *antibiotics* may not cure or control them. Blood, which carries medication, doesn't flow through cartilage, so there is simply no way to get powerful drugs to the infection site. That leaves the germs free to go on damaging tissue. If you have ever seen a boxer with a "cauliflower" ear, then you know what the end result of this kind of problem can look like. It's even worse if an infection gets into your nose cartilage.

Piercings can also cause *keloids* to form. Keloids are large, thick, ugly scars that can continue growing indefinitely. When you remove them, they often come back even larger. For some unknown reason, the area in and around your navel has the highest risk for keloid formation. Keloids can occur anywhere on the body and are very difficult to treat. If you have a family member with keloids or have developed one yourself, think twice about getting piercings or tattoos.

Allergies can also be an issue. Many people are sensitive to nickel or brass, and jewelry often contains these metals. If your piercing is constantly inflamed or swollen, this may be your problem. Here are the metals least likely to cause an allergic reaction:

> ▸ **Implant-grade stainless steel.** This metal is the least likely of all to cause complications.
> ▸ **Gold.** Use at least 18 karat gold in a new piercing, and 14 karat in one that has healed.
> ▸ **Silver.** Silver is a good choice for healed piercings. Avoid it with new ones, as it can leave tarnish on the skin around the wound. Sterling silver may contain nickel, a hardening metal, so avoid this if you know you have a nickel allergy.
> ▸ **Titanium and niobium.** These metals are somewhat expensive, but good choices for both new and healed piercings.

Piercing Care

Giving your new piercing proper care is important both to encourage healing and to prevent complications such as infection. First, the wound may become slightly swollen over the first couple of days. This is normal. Also, fluid from the wound may form a little crust on the new jewelry. You can clean it off with warm water. Otherwise, here is what to do:

- ▸ **"Hands off".** You may be tempted to twist, rub, or otherwise play with your newly installed jewelry. Don't. It will increase *inflammation* and expose the wound to infection.

- ▸ **Wash.** Wash your hands with soap and water before you clean the piercing.

- ▸ **Prevent snags.** Keep clothing clear of your new piercing. It can snag the jewelry or cause rubbing and chaffing problems.

- ▸ **Suck ice.** If you experience pain and swelling after a tongue piercing, sucking on ice cubes can help, but you may also need to see a doctor for some anti-inflammatory medicine.

- ▸ **Rinse your mouth.** To keep oral piercings clean while they heal, use an anti-bacterial, alcohol-free mouthwash after meals and before bedtime. Also, get a new toothbrush—one with soft bristles. Your old brush contains germs you don't want in your piercing.

- ▸ **Cleanse.** Remove crusting with warm water and a cotton ball or sterile tissue. Use a liquid medicated cleanser around the piercing. It's okay to twist the jewelry a little to work the cleanser into the opening of the wound. Do *not* use alcohol, peroxide, or ointments.

- ▸ **Know when to worry.** If extreme swelling, yellow or green drainage, or fever occurs, see your doctor.

Tattoos. If you have never seen anyone actually getting a tattoo, here is what happens: The tattoo artist uses a machine that supplies a handheld needle with pigments of various colors. The needle rapidly pricks the skin over and over, like a sewing machine, injecting permanent dye into the upper layer of the skin. It is a tedious and painful process, but some people want tattoos badly enough to tolerate the discomfort.

As with piercings, tattooing has its risks. For one thing, no one regulates what goes into the ink, so you're never quite sure what is going into your body. It is not uncommon, for example, to receive dye that has very tiny bits of metal it—especially in the red colors. Under most circumstances, this wouldn't really matter, as the metal doesn't travel below the skin barrier. But it can matter a great deal if you need a type of X-ray called an MRI, as the metal will heat up and can cause uncomfortable swelling and intense burning. In some cases, it can also reduce the quality of the image, and that can make diagnosis more difficult.

As with piercings, tattoos expose you to a risk for skin infections and bloodborne diseases, although these complications are rare these days. The risk that you might be allergic to metal in the dye, however, is real and serious. Here are some of the metals in tattoo ink that cause problems:

> Mercury sulfide (red ink)
> Chromium and chromic oxide (green ink)
> Cobalt albuminate (blue ink)
> Cadmium (yellow ink)

The problem with being allergic to tattoo ink, of course, is that it's fixed permanently under your skin. Reactions can cause intense burning, itching, swelling, and disfigurement. Not a pretty picture, and the discomfort can go on for months—however long it takes for your body to break down the offending substance. In some cases, the inflammation is so severe that the tattoo must be surgically removed.

Tattoos can also give rise to keloids, as well as permanent bumps, called *granulomas,* that form around the ink.

If despite all of the risks involved you still decide to get a tattoo, there are some things you can do to protect yourself. To begin with, make certain the artist has a license or certificate to practice in your area. Also, follow your intuition. If you walk into a tattoo parlor and it doesn't seem clean or the employees strike you in any way as behaving unprofessionally, walk out.

Precautions regarding cleanliness during the procedure are extremely important. First of all, the needle, tubes, dye, trays, and containers should all be fresh and unused from the package. All other equipment should be sterilized in an *autoclave,* a machine

Are Tattoos Reversible?

Tattooing is not designed for temporary ornamentation. It puts permanent ink deep into the skin, all the way down in the dermis, where the cells are stable and hold the colors in place over a lifetime. Unfortunately, after a few years, the inks can move a little, their brilliance fades, and of course, your skin may stretch and wrinkle, so the look of the drawing can change and even distort. So if a tattoo gradually loses its attractiveness—or if the wearer just decides he or she doesn't want it any more—can it be removed? Yes and no. Pulsed lasers are the most common method of removing tattoos, but the process is expensive, painful, and doesn't completely get rid of all of the color. Here is how it works: Lasers are highly focused beams of light that carry a lot of energy. Certain wavelengths of that light can go through the upper layer of your skin and straight to the dermis, where the tattoo dyes absorb them. The energy in the lasers causes the dye particles to break up into much smaller pieces, which the immune system can then dissolve. Removal is not a one-step process. You will have to undergo the treatment several times before it is finished, and some ink always remains behind. Pulsed lasers may also damage the skin, so you may end up with some scarring. As for those tattoo-removal creams you see advertised on the Internet, so far, there is no reliable evidence that they work.

If you are considering a tattoo, ask about removable tattoo ink. With this new ink technology, one or two laser treatments can erase the tattoo. Temporary tattoos can also be applied with henna or vegetable dyes. Consider these options before making a choice you will have to live with for the rest of your life.

designed for that purpose. Finally, everything else in the room that people touch should be cleaned with disinfectant after every customer.

The tattooist should thoroughly scrub his or her hands and put on a new pair of latex gloves before starting the procedure. If the gloves accidentally touch any surface other than the instruments and your skin, they should be changed.

WHAT YOU NEED TO KNOW

➤ The skin is an external organ of the integumentary system, which protects your inner organs from contact with the outside environment, maintains body temperature, and allows you to feel the sensation of touch.

➤ The skin is composed of three layers: the dermis, the epidermis, and the subcutaneous layer.

➤ Some skin conditions appear at puberty as a result of hormonal changes, including acne, excessive sweating, and unwanted hair growth. While these conditions are unsightly, nearly everybody experiences at least one of them.

➤ Some skin conditions, such as psoriasis, ichthyosis, vitiligo, and excessive moles can be genetic.

➤ Sports, risky behaviors, and skin to skin contact with other people can all lead to various skin problems, including injuries and infection.

➤ Good skin care includes cleansing once a day with a mild, neutral soap and lukewarm water, applying a moisturizer, and avoiding the sun and tanning lamps.

➤ Piercings and tattoos expose you to the risk of infections, granulomas, and keloids.

➤ Make certain that anyone who pierces your skin with a piece of jewelry or tattoo needle is certified or licensed, that his or her workspace is clean, and all instruments are sterilized.

2 ▮▮

A Personal Plan to Deal with Acne

Ashley, at 14, could hardly imagine how her life could be worse. First, her parents separated. Then, after they sold their split-level home in the suburbs, she had to leave behind all of her childhood friends—including Humphrey the Basset Hound—to move with her mother to a small apartment across town. Finally, when she had to start at a new school—without a single person to hang out with or confide in—she thought she'd finally sunk as low as a person could go.

Now she knew she had been wrong. Examining her face in the mirror this morning before her first day of classes, she realized she had been nowhere near the bottom before today. Because *this*—the reflection looking back at her—was the bottom.

For most of Ashley's life, adults had complimented her luxurious, long, copper red hair, blue eyes, and most of all, her "peaches and cream" complexion. Lately—at least before she moved—boys had been noticing her as well. But they wouldn't now, she thought. They wouldn't even give her a second look because that pretty, clear, soft skin was no more. In its place were a forehead and cheeks full of pimples. She tried to cover them with thick pancake makeup, but it just didn't work. She could hide the red color, but the bumps remained. She did not want to go to school looking this way. And anyway, her mother would never know if she skipped. She had already left for work. And even if she found out, so what? It didn't matter. Nothing mattered if you had to go through life looking as if you'd just been stung by a swarm of hornets. Ashley made up her mind. In this condition, she would never leave the apartment. Never.

Acne vulgaris, also known simply as acne, is an affliction that nearly everyone copes with at some point in his or her life. For many, it's an occasional, minor annoyance. For others, it's a nightmare that can leave both physical and emotional scars that last a long, long time. In either case, acne has a way of always showing up at the worst possible time. It struck Ashley, for example, when she was feeling extraordinarily vulnerable, her life seemed totally out of control, and hormonal changes in her body were causing her endless havoc and confusion.

Whether Ashley's condition becomes a major problem or a minor annoyance might well depend on what she does next to treat it. Using inexpensive over-the-counter medications and proper skin care may improve it in a few weeks' time. If that doesn't work, or if she develops an extreme form of the condition, she may need to see a *dermatologist,* who will have a whole arsenal of treatments to defend against the acne beast. But if she does nothing at all, or worse, aggravates her condition by doing all the wrong things—picking at the pimples or overcleaning with harsh soaps—she may make the situation worse.

THE REAL FACE OF ACNE

Although acne is one of the most common skin problems that doctors see, it is also one of the most misunderstood by the public. For example, many people, including moms and dads, believe that dirt causes pimples. It doesn't. And washing won't make them go away. The fact is, acne starts under the surface of the skin, where neither dirt nor soap and water can reach. (Remember, the skin isn't a sponge—it's not built to absorb substances. It's built to keep them out.)

Skin Facts: Did You Know?

Some 42 million people in the United States have acne. That's more people than the entire population of California. Although full-blown acne occurs more often among teens than other age groups, occasional small papules and comedones are common by age seven.

Many people also believe that certain foods, such as chocolate, sodas, sugar, or French fries, can cause an acne outbreak. While these they may not be great for your teeth—or your weight—they don't put you in danger of skin eruptions. Because teens, who experience more acne than other age groups, also tend to consume a lot of snacks rich in fat and sugar, it's easy to assume a cause-and-effect connection, but there is no direct relationship.

Then what does cause the problem? To begin with, a group of hormones called *androgens* increase dramatically as you go through puberty, triggering your body to move from childhood to adulthood. Unfortunately, they can also trigger acne to form.

Androgens are important. If you're a boy, they help you become stronger, fill out in the muscular shape of a young man, grow taller and heavier, make your voice lower, and help develop mature reproductive organs. They also stimulate hair growth on your face and body and increase the number of red cells in your blood.

If you're a girl, they make you taller, stimulate your breasts to grow and hips to widen, give you underarm and pubic hair, cause you to have periods (*menstruate*), and help your reproductive system mature so that it's possible for you to bear children. For both boys and girls, androgens stimulate you emotionally to become more independent in the way you think and feel.

On the downside, whether you're male or female, they can make you sweat more, give you body odor, and cause your sebaceous glands to produce more oil. It's that last effect, increased oil production—with help from a bacteria called *Propionibacterium acnes* (*P. acnes*)—that causes acne to flare. That's also why acne tends to occur where you have the highest number of sebaceous glands: the face, neck, shoulders, chest, and back.

An acne flare actually starts in your skin's pores. Under each pore's opening is a shaft that contains a hair. Together, the hair, shaft, and

Skin Facts: Did You Know?

Blackheads are dark in color because of the way in which sebum and dead skin cells react with the oxygen in the air as they reach the surface. They are not plugs of "dirt" that can be washed away.

the sebaceous gland connecting to the hair shaft are called a *pilose-baceous unit.* The glands produce an oil, *sebum,* which lubricates the hair and skin.

When your body begins producing androgens at puberty, they stimulate the glands to secrete a lot more oil. They also cause the pores to speed up production of new skin cells in the walls of the follicle shaft. The new cells force old, dead ones to fall off. These dead cells mix with the sebum, making a thick, sticky paste, like when you combine water and flour to make dough. Eventually, the concoction forms a plug that blocks the pore. Plugged pores are called *comedones.* When the plug remains below the surface of the skin, it is called a closed comedone and appears as a whitehead. If it works its way to surface, you end up with an open comedone—a blackhead.

In some people, acne remains at this relatively mild stage, although someone coping with blackheads and whiteheads might not think of his or her situation as mild. As you probably know, however, the situation can get worse. These comedones can go on to develop into red pimples, and, in the worst cases, become cysts that can leave scars behind.

Red pimples develop as a result of inflammation, and inflammation happens when *P. acnes* bacteria overgrows in a plugged pore, causing a *papule* (a little, red raised spot) or a *pustule* (bump with pus in it). In *nodulocystic acne,* the infection actually causes the follicle to burst or collapse beneath the skin's surface, and the infection, along with inflammation and pus, spreads into the surrounding tissue, creating more inflammation and, possibly, a scar.

AN OUNCE OF PREVENTION: WHAT TO AVOID

With all of this talk about androgens, comedones, and inflammation, it may sound as if there is nothing you can do to defend yourself against acne flares—especially now that you know that washing your face and avoiding chocolate doesn't help. Not so. It is true that the grade of acne you develop—mild, moderate, or severe—depends somewhat upon genes you have inherited from your parents. That's one part of the picture you can't change. However, there is still a lot you can do—and avoid doing—to keep your acne flares to a minimum.

First, here are some activities you should definitely avoid:

Scrubbing hard. When you scrub your skin as if you're trying to remove a spot from a shirt, you irritate it, and irritation, as we've said

When Is "Acne" Not Acne?

Not everything that looks like an acne breakout really is one, so be sure to see a doctor if your over-the-counter medication doesn't work after a couple of months. Here are some conditions that can do a very good job of imitating acne:

Folliculitis. This is an infection of a hair follicle, often caused by a bacteria called *Staphylococcus.* You may need a prescription of oral or topical antibiotics to cure it.

Milia. These are tiny cysts that appear on the face and resemble whiteheads. If they bother you, your doctor may be able to remove them or treat them with a topical retinoid cream or gel.

Perioral dermatitis. This is a rash that appears around your mouth and sometimes around your nose and eyes. It can be bumpy and scaly, and it can come and go on its own. It can be a result of topical *corticosteroid* use.

Keratosis pilaris. This condition often appears on the cheeks, upper arms, buttocks, and thighs. It looks like "goose flesh" and may feel rough like sandpaper when you rub your hand over it. Your doctor can help you find a treatment.

Adenoma sebaceum (angiofibromas). These are firm red or brown papules that appear on your chin and cheeks. They result from a genetic disorder. Your doctor can help you with treatment.

before, is another word for inflammation. That's the very reaction that causes acne in the first place. So if you're trying to remove blackheads with a rough washcloth, you may actually be inviting them to turn into papules and pustules. For some teens, using *exfoliants* and getting facials can have the same unwanted effects.

Picking, pinching, and squeezing. If you have pustules, especially on your face, you may feel a great temptation simply to squeeze and pop them. This is really not a good idea. The problem is that every time you pop a pimple, some of the stuff inside of it, including bacteria, shoots back into your skin and causes more inflammation. It's the same thing that happens when a follicle ruptures on its own, and it will increase the chance that your pimple will leave a scar.

Going too snug. You may notice that anything irritating or rubbing your skin can make you break out. Among the common irritants are clothes or sporting equipment that fit too tightly. A tight jogging bra or a football helmet, for example, can rub and cause friction on areas of your skin, especially when you're sweating heavily. The result? Irritation and pimples. This doesn't mean you have to give up sports or exercise. It just means that you should wear clothing and equipment that fit properly and don't chafe.

Wearing thick makeup. Heavy foundation makeup or even a thick moisturizer can worsen acne, so when you're shopping at the drugstore, you need to take a little time and choose noncomedogenic, oil-free products. That means the formulation is less likely to cause an acne breakout. There are many great brands to choose from, and most are inexpensive.

Using steroids. Hormones are very powerful chemicals that stimulate various cells and organs in your body to behave in specific ways. *Anabolic steroids*—the ones body builders and athletes use to grow bigger muscles or develop more strength—are either *testosterone* or testosterone-like substances, all of which are androgens. If you recall, androgens are the culprits behind acne flares—and that's why using steroids is like issuing an invitation to pimples to have a party on your skin. Anabolic steroids are also illegal and can harm your health in other, very serious ways. Your best bet? Leave these substances alone. Whatever small benefits they may offer in muscle strength are more than offset by the price you'll pay in poor health.

Taking acne-genic medications. Unfortunately, some drugs that can be very helpful when you're sick can also create havoc with your skin. These include seizure medications and a few of the medications for psychological or emotional problems such as depression. They also include anti-inflammatory medications that contain steroids, such as those you might use to control asthma. These steroids, also called corticosteroids, are not the same as those used by athletes and bodybuilders. Either type, however, can cause inflammatory acne lesions. A word of caution is important here: Never, ever stop taking prescription medication without first talking it over with your doctor.

If you need a particular drug to stay healthy, giving it up to avoid a breakout is not a good idea. Your doctor can treat your acne or change your medication to one that causes less acne. The important thing to remember here is that this is a situation for you and your doctor to handle as a team.

SITUATION HOPEFUL: WHAT YOU CAN DO

Even when you've done everything to prevent breakouts, sometimes they happen anyway, which can be aggravating, discouraging, and depressing. Don't give up hope. You can do a lot to keep the problem under control. In fact, you can start right now. Here is what to do.

Step 1: Give your acne a grade. Acne basically falls into three broad grades: mild, moderate, and severe, with many cases falling somewhere in between. While you would need to see your family doctor or a dermatologist to get an actual diagnosis, a close look in the mirror can give you a good idea of which group your lesions fall into. Here's what to look for:

- ➤ **Mild:** Comedones (blackheads and whiteheads only)
- ➤ **Mild to moderate:** Comedones and a few papules and pustules (inflamed pimples)
- ➤ **Moderate:** Many papules, pustules, and comedones
- ➤ **Severe:** Papules and pustules with cysts, possibly widespread with or without scarring

Step 2: Choose your approach. This is the simplest part of the process because it depends entirely on the results of step 1. If you graded your acne as severe, then you need to see your family doctor, or better yet, a dermatologist to help you bring it under control. With any other grade, you can try remedies that are available without a prescription from your local drugstore.

However, even though this step is simple, it is not necessarily easy. It requires a commitment and real action. Treatment will not work unless you do it daily and correctly, not just when your acne flares. If you're going to try self-treatment, get to the nearest pharmacy today or tomorrow, and find the medications that are right for your acne type. (More on those later.) If you need to see a doctor, call one as soon as possible—many doctors schedule appointments months in advance. And make sure to keep the appointment, even if your acne seems to get better while you are waiting.

Step 3: Stick to your plan. Acne treatment usually means applying some form of medication to your skin. For some people, it also involves taking pills. Whatever you need to do, do it each and every day. If you're using nonprescription medications, read the directions and follow them correctly. If your doctor has prescribed drugs for you, use them exactly as instructed. Many teens find this a real challenge. Some give up entirely. Don't be one of them. Fighting acne requires stamina, determination, and patience, but you can do it. Having patience may be the most frustrating part. When pimples show up, you want them gone immediately. In fact, yesterday wouldn't be soon enough. Unfortunately, no matter what the TV, radio, and magazine ads might say, there is no overnight fix for pimples. Most medications, whether they're prescription drugs or over-the-counter remedies, take from two to three months to work. So start out on the right foot by making a promise to yourself. Put it in writing—in your diary or journal or just a piece of paper that is for you, and only you, to see. Or, have a conversation with yourself in the mirror. Either way, promise yourself that you're going to make a plan to treat your skin, and then stick with it.

SELF-TREATMENT WITH OVER-THE-COUNTER MEDICATION

Nearly seven out of 10 teens who treat their acne use nonprescription products applied directly to the skin. For mild and many moderate cases, these remedies can be very effective. They come in packages of many sizes and shapes, but basically, they all contain the same effective medication: *benzoyl peroxide.* Brand names include Clearasil, Clearplex, DermSelect, Desquam-E, Fostex, PanOxyl, and Oxy.

Benzoyl peroxide acts as an anti-inflammatory, so it's mainly good for red papules and pustules—in other words, pimples. It works by decreasing bacteria and fatty acids on the skin, and it also helps unplug pores. It comes in a number of different forms and different strengths:

> ➤ **Shaving creams.** Apply to affected area once a day.
> ➤ **Facial mask.** Use once a week or as your doctor directs.
> ➤ **Gels, creams, and lotions.** Apply to affected areas of skin once or twice a day.
> ➤ **Pads containing liquids or solutions.** Apply once or twice a day.
> ➤ **Soaps and washes.** Use once or twice a day. You likely need to leave these types on for five minutes or so.
> ➤ **Sticks.** Apply to affected areas once to three times a day.

Tips for Managing Your Acne

Here are a few tips to help you stick with your treatment plan:

Make smart decisions. Before choosing a plan, talk with your doctor or pharmacist about what each medication does. Then, based on what you learn, make a decision as to which are right for you. Smearing yourself with a cream or swallowing pills every day becomes easier if you know exactly how these medications are helping you. You're also more likely to stick with your daily treatment if you have some say in deciding what will go into it.

Add your acne meds to your other routines. Apply or take your meds when you're doing other regular, daily activities. For example, if you're taking pills twice a day, then do it after breakfast and dinner (check with a pharmacist to make sure that it's okay to take your medication right after you eat). If you're applying ointments or creams, do it right after your shower in the morning and right before dinner. Applying creams at bedtime works for some people, but many, including adults, tend to forget their medications when they're tired and preparing for sleep. If it works for you, keep your acne cream next to your toothbrush. When you brush your teeth at night, apply your cream.

Give yourself hints. Set your medications out where you can't miss them, or set a daily calendar nearby to remind you to use your acne medicines. If you hide them in a medicine cabinet or a drawer, you might easily forget to take them out, especially if your mind is on other things.

Use combinations. Your doctor can prescribe some acne products that offer two different active medications combined into one mixture. The fewer steps you have in your routine, the less likely you are to put off or skip applications and doses.

Each form has its advantages and disadvantages. Gels dry out oily skin but may sting dry skin. Creams have some moisturizing effect, but may also leave a greasy residue. Lotions are easy to apply, but again, many are greasy. Solutions (applied with sponge or pad) are easy to apply and leave no residue, but can cause dry skin. Cleansers are also easy to apply, but they don't remain on your skin for very long.

Follow directions on the package to the letter. Don't add any extra applications to your routine, and use only the amount you need to cover the affected area. More does not equal better—in fact, increasing your dosage may actually cause skin irritation and dryness.

For gels, creams, masks, pads, sticks, and lotions, wash the affected area of skin with a mild soap and gently pat it dry with a clean towel before applying the medication. Apply the product in a thin layer to your entire face (chest and back too, if you have acne there). Don't just spot treat your pimples with a benzoyl peroxide product. The goal is to clear up what you have and prevent new pimples from forming. You shouldn't allow benzoyl peroxide to come into contact with your eyes, lips, or the inside of your mouth or nose. It can be irritating to your skin, even when used correctly. If benzoyl peroxide gets on your towels, clothing, or sheets, it will leave bleach stains.

SOME BASIC PRECAUTIONS

If you are using prescription creams on your face for eczema or another condition, check with your doctor first before starting over-the-counter treatments for acne. Some acne medication may irritate the skin and make your eczema worse.

Use an acne product and a mild soap for washing your face. Stay away from any skin products that might be irritating, such as after-shave lotion, rubbing alcohol, and astringents. Many over-the-counter products contain exfoliators (alpha hydroxy acid, glycolic acid, beta hydroxy acid, salicylic acid), generally in nonirritating amounts, so they're okay to use. These work by increasing the rate at which you

Skin Facts: Did You Know?

Frequent spot treatments for pimples, such as dabbing them with toothpaste, don't really help and may make the situation worse by irritating your skin even more.

shed the top layer of your skin, which unplugs your pores. *Retinoids,* prescription medications that will be discussed later, also exfoliate and do a much better job than the over-the-counter choices.

There are a few issues to think about when using over-the-counter medications. Your acne may actually get worse before it starts getting better, and it may take four to six weeks before you start seeing any result. If after that time you haven't seen any improvement, you should consult with a doctor. Also, some people are allergic to benzoyl peroxide—but these allergies are very rare.

PARTNERING WITH YOUR DOCTOR

A doctor can be your new best friend in your fight against acne. He or she has a lot of experience in treating acne and can help you with a treatment plan that exactly fits your needs. A physician can also write prescriptions, which means a much wider range of treatments for you. You'll also have a valuable resource in knowing that someone understands what you're going through at every level—physical and emotional—and can answer any question you might have about your condition.

For acne treatment, you'll want to see your family doctor, your pediatrician, or a specialist called a *dermatologist.* The advantage in seeing your family doctor or pediatrician is that he or she already knows you and may have taken care of all your illnesses from the day you were born. It's always easier to work with someone with whom you feel comfortable and familiar, and these kinds of doctors see enough cases of acne to have a lot of practical ideas about how to treat it.

When you see a specialist, on the other hand, you're working with someone who is the real expert in your specific condition. He or she will know what to do if the first treatments you try don't work and will have a lot more experience treating cases of really severe acne. If you see an even more specialized specialist, called a pediatric dermatologist, you'll have someone on your team who is an acne expert and really understands teenagers. They have trained in both pediatrics and dermatology after medical school. If you would like to see one of these specialists, talk with your primary-care physician about referring you to one.

In working with your doctor, it's important to understand that you're more than just a patient: You're a partner in managing your treatment. Both of you are working toward the same goal, and you should be thinking together about how to reach that goal. For your part, if there is anything you don't understand or would like to know more about, you need to speak up. If you're uncomfortable with something the doctor recommends for treatment, for example, say so in a respectful way. If you know why you feel this way, explain that as well. Then the two of you can discuss your issues and resolve them. It's also important to be honest. If you haven't been using your medications as you should, don't lie about it. After all, it's not like you're going to get into trouble. And having the facts out in the open will help the doctor make some judgments about what steps to take next. In fact, together you may be able to come with some ideas for helping you stick to your acne-fighting routine.

You Should See a Doctor If:

▸ Using over-the-counter medication doesn't help after two months.

▸ Your pimples are leaving scars on your skin.

▸ You have large bumps (cysts) under your skin.

▸ Your acne seems to be getting worse, despite all your efforts.

YOUR FIRST DOCTOR VISIT

The first time you see a doctor for acne, you will probably have to answer a few questions to help him or her get a better idea of what you're coping with. Here are some topics you will probably touch on:

Severity. The doctor will determine this by examining your acne and giving it a grade of mild, moderate, severe, or somewhere in between.

Duration. This just means the length of time that you've been dealing with acne. This information may help your doctor identify the most effective treatments for you.

Medication. If you're now using or have ever used any over-the-counter or prescription medications for acne, let the doctor know. Also, be prepared to tell him or her how well the medicines did—or didn't—work. Your doctor will want to know if you've had irritation (redness and peeling) when using acne products in the past. This will help point the way to the right routine for your skin type. If you're taking medications for any reason other than acne, you should let the doctor know about those also. They may not mix well with acne drugs.

Family history. Like many medical conditions, acne tends to run in families. In fact, scientists recently discovered that substances made by some particular genes show up in much higher than normal amounts in acne lesions. Genes are tiny structures in your cells that carry all of the traits you inherited from your parents, grandparents, and ancestors. By learning about other acne cases in your family, your doctor may come to a better understanding of your own case. In particular, he or she will want to know if either of your parents or any of your brothers or sisters have acne scars. That will help determine if you're at risk for them as well, which in turn will help both you and your doctor choose a medication that can help prevent that from happening.

Hormones. Hormones, as we've seen, can have a powerful impact on your skin, so your doctor will want to know how yours have been behaving. If you're a girl and you have noticeable hair on your upper lip, chin, chest, neck, or back, you may have an excess of androgens circulating in your blood. Irregular periods can also be a sign that your hormonal picture is slightly out of balance. Your doctor may also ask if you're on birth control pills. It's important that you be honest in your answer. The pills contain female hormones, which may be having an effect on your skin—often a positive effect.

Cosmetics. The makeup you put on your face and products you put into your hair can affect the way your skin behaves. Using non-comedogenic products may go a long way toward controlling your breakout problems.

TOPICAL MEDICATION

Once your doctor has the information he or she needs, the next step will be to discuss your treatment options. Generally, for mild to moderate acne—comedones and pimples—topical medicines such as lotions, gels, creams, pads, washes, and soaps will be your best bet. For more severe cases, you may need to take some medicine by mouth as well.

All medications have side effects, some more severe than others. To avoid them, follow your doctors instructions closely when using your medicine. If you notice your body giving you any unusual signs—*nausea*, vomiting, abdominal pain, rashes, or anything else—contact your doctor right away.

All of the acne medications mentioned below are listed by their common *generic* name. There are many brand names, and new ones are constantly appearing on the market. Your doctor may prescribe a generic version of your medicines, which means simply that there is no brand name on the package, and it sells at a lower price. In most cases, it is exactly the same or very similar to the brand. So if you find yourself using tretinoin rather than Retin-A, for example, you're still getting the good stuff. Be aware, however, that many acne products, especially combination ones, do not come in a generic version and can be expensive because of that.

Benzoyl peroxide. If you're already using benzoyl peroxide, your doctor may want you to continue doing so, although he or she may want to adjust the strength of the medication or add other medications to it. There are many products on the market to choose from, depending on your skin type (oily or dry) and preferences for use (e.g., washing once daily or applying gel at night).

The most common side effect is skin irritation such as stinging, redness, peeling, or burning. This will improve with time and a non-comedogenic face lotion may help.

Topical antibiotics. These are prescription medicines that can help kill the bacteria that contribute to acne. Most topical antibiotics contain either *clindamycin* or *erythromycin* and come in lotions, solutions, foams, and pads. This type of acne medication can really help bring a persistent case under control, but it's important to use it until your doctor says it's okay to stop, even if your skin clears up. Most doctors will also prescribe a benzoyl peroxide product for patients using topical antibiotics to prevent skin bacteria from becoming resistant to treatment.

The most common side effect of topical antibiotics is skin irritation with itching, stinging, or burning, and this generally isn't serious. However, in very rare cases, you can be allergic to the antibiotic, and more serious symptoms can occur. If you notice anything unusual—a rash, swelling in your face or lips, tightness in your chest, or anything else out of the ordinary—contact your doctor immediately.

Retinoids. These are chemical relatives of vitamin A. They are useful because they are *keratolytic,* which means that they increase the rate of skin cell shedding from the uppermost layer of your skin, allowing replacement layers to move into place more quickly. As you're shedding and replacing cells, you're also unplugging pores, so this is a great treatment for stubborn blackheads and whiteheads and can also be helpful in moderate to severe acne. Three types of retinoids are available: *tretinoin, adapalene,* and *tazarotene.* Your doctor will know which type is right for you.

The most important and common side effect of retinoids is skin irritation. When first using these products, start with every-other-day application, and increase to daily use as tolerated over two to three weeks. A pea-sized amount is plenty to treat your face. More will only irritate your skin. Retinoids may also make you more sensitive to the sun. Wear a noncomedogenic face lotion daily with an SPF rating of 15 or more while using topical retinoids.

Combination products. Some products combine two topical medications together into one product. These meds are a good idea for many teens, as they cut down the number of applications you need to remember. Most will contain either a combination of benzoyl peroxide and antibiotic, retinoid and antibiotic, or retinoid and benzoyl peroxide. Together, these products will probably work better than a single product alone. For example, benzoyl peroxide with antibiotics penetrate the skin better, kill more bacteria, and aren't as likely to create antibiotic-resistant germs, while retinol and antibiotic combinations help prevent comedones from forming, kill bacteria, and reduce

At-A-Glance Treatments

Severity	Treatment	Action
Mild: Blackheads/ whiteheads	Benzoyl peroxide (topical)	Reduces inflammation, fights bacteria
	Exfoliants (topical)	Unplugs pores, speeds up skin-shedding cycle
Moderate: Papules/pustules	Benzoyl peroxide (topical)	Reduces inflammation, fights bacteria
	Antibiotics (topical)	Kills bacteria in follicles and on skin
	Retinoids (topical)	Unplugs pores, speeds up skin-shedding cycle
	Antibiotics (oral)	Kills bacteria in follicles and on skin
	Hormonal Medication (oral)	Reduces acne-causing androgens
Severe: Cysts/scars	All of the above	
	Isotretinoin (oral)	Reduces sebum, makes cells less sticky, and fights bacteria

inflammation. Side effects for these products include all of those for either product alone.

ORAL MEDICATION

If you have severe acne—cysts and nodules—taking oral medications can help bring it under control. Oral medications affect your body's entire system, so if you have side effects, they are more likely to show up in places other than acne-affected areas of skin. Here are some oral medications that doctors prescribe.

Oral antibiotics. Just like their topical cousins, oral antibiotics kill germs, but they do it from the inside out. Your bloodstream carries

Skin Facts: Did You Know?

Sixteen percent of all teens with acne use prescription drugs in their treatment.

them to the site in your skin where they can complete their mission. These drugs are especially effective for moderate-to-severe acne that affects a large area or when topical therapies alone just do not work. Often, your doctor will want you to use a benzyl peroxide soap or cream along with your antibiotics to help keep the bacteria from developing resistance to the drugs. The most effective oral antibiotics fall into a family called the *tetracyclines,* which include tetracycline, *doxycycline,* and *minocycline.* With some patients, such as people who are allergic to tetracyclines, doctors use other types of antibiotic such as *cephalexin, erythromycin,* or others. Most of these medicines require that you take a pill twice daily. The dose depends upon your weight. Tetracycline needs to be taken on an empty stomach for better absorption into your body. The others can be taken with meals.

Side effects of antibiotic use can include upset stomach, vomiting, diarrhea, and allergic reactions (hives and swelling). For doxycyline in particular, severe *photosensitivity* (easy sunburning) can become a problem.

Oral contraceptives. It may sound strange, but birth control pills can be very effective in helping girls control their acne, especially those who don't respond to antibiotics. They work by lowering your androgen production and raising your levels of female hormones. Unfortunately, some teens—and some parents of teens—are so put off by the idea of a 12- or 13-year-old girl using contraceptives that they refuse this kind of treatment. In fact, these medications are really "contraceptives" only when they're used to prevent pregnancies. The United States Food and Drug Administration, however, has approved them for another use: treating acne. So in this case, we don't think of them as birth control pills, because they're not being taken to prevent pregnancy. Instead, we call them what they are: hormonal acne treatments. Because they have fewer risks and side effects, these pills are generally considered a safer treatment than the next drug you will learn about, *isotretinoin* (Accutane and others), and in some cases can make the use of isotretinoin unnecessary.

Side effects can include breakthrough bleeding and a small amount of weight gain, but usually there are none. Your doctor would review side effects in detail with you and your parents before starting this hormone treatment.

Isotretinoin (brand names Accutane, Sotret, Claravis, Amnesteem). This is the most effective treatment we have for acne. It's different from other retinoids in that it comes in pill form rather than a cream. It works by making sebaceous glands smaller and decreasing their output of oil. It also makes dead skin cells less sticky so they don't clump together as much, and it fights bacteria in the sebaceous gland and on the skin's surface. So if it's so great, why don't we give it to everyone? Two words: side effects. It can severely dry out your skin and *mucous membranes* (the skin on the inside of your lips, mouth, and nose), making them sore, chapped, and irritated. It can also raise certain fats, called *triglycerides,* to unhealthful levels in your bloodstream. Your doctor has to monitor these and other potential side effects closely during therapy. Worst of all, if you're pregnant, isotretinoin is almost certain to cause your unborn baby to develop birth defects. It can also cause the baby to come too early (*premature birth*), die in the womb (*miscarriage*), or die shortly after birth. If you're pregnant or think you may become pregnant in the next few months, you absolutely cannot take isotretinoin. You also can't use it if you are breast-feeding.

There are a few more precautions you need to take when you're on this medicine. First, do not donate your blood. It will contain significant amounts of the medication, and if given to a pregnant woman, will have a strong chance of causing birth defects. Second, for your own safety, stay out of the sun as much as possible while you're on isotretinoin and under no circumstances spend any time in a tanning bed. The medication will make your skin overly sensitive to ultraviolet radiation, the type of light that causes tans and sunburns.

Finally, some people believe that isotretinoin can cause serious mental health problems, including depression and suicidal thoughts. Your doctor will discuss this possibility with you and your parents. If you're taking the drug, you and your parents will watch for signs of moodiness and depression and should let your doctor know about these changes. Many teenagers report feeling better during and after treatment with isotretinoin. As acne improves, often so does self-esteem.

Only teens who have severe acne are candidates for isotretinoin, and all of these must join the iPLEDGE program. The program outlines a series of steps that doctors, patients, and pharmacists must follow during isotretinoin treatment. Both girls and boys in the program must be able to keep once-a-month appointments with their doctors. Isotretinoin is never prescribed for more than 30 days at a time, so if you can't show up at your physician's office every month, you won't be able to get your medicine.

Because the main purpose of iPLEDGE is to prevent pregnancies that could lead to birth defects, girls in the program have additional steps to follow. First, you will have to choose and use two *effective* forms of birth control, starting one month before you begin taking isotretinoin. Since not all forms of birth control are considered effective, your doctor can help you choose which methods would be right for you. You will also have to take either a blood or urine pregnancy test every month. Your doctor has to submit the results of these tests to the iPLEDGE system before you will be allowed to renew your prescription. You may also have to answer some questions from iPLEDGE and confirm the types of birth control that you're using. For more information, an online iPLEDGE brochure is available at www. ipledgeprogram.com.

THE EMOTIONAL SIDE OF ACNE

Remember 14-year-old Ashley? When she had her breakout, she could barely bring herself to leave the house. At a time when everything in her life seemed to be changing—new home, new school, new people, living with only one parent—she felt that her body had betrayed her and turned her into the most unattractive, unlovable person in the world. Her reaction isn't unusual. Acne, especially if it's severe, can make you feel that your life is completely ruined.

Unfortunately, there are some parents—and other adults—who aren't always sensitive to this. Perhaps they have forgotten what it's like to go through a sudden change in appearance and the feelings of shame that go with it. Maybe they just chalk every feeling you have up to "adolescence" and don't seem to take you seriously, or they give you lectures about how being a beautiful person on the inside is what is really important in life—which you already know, but you also know that isn't the issue here. On the other hand, you might be someone who keeps some emotions hidden inside, so your parents may not know what your feelings really are.

The truth is that having acne can be very hard, and if you have a really bad case that leaves scars, it can be devastating. After all, we live in a culture that glamorizes the quest for beauty and perfection. You see it in films, television, and magazines and in the huge number of cosmetic products people buy to look more attractive. And you see it in all the attention that goes to the best-looking kids at school. In the midst of all of this, acne can make you feel as if you have nothing to look forward to in your life but rejection and loneliness.

It should come as no surprise, then, that teens with acne are more prone to depression, anxiety, and withdrawal from their friends and family. It can have a negative impact on their studies and job performance. Many who try to do something about it with over-the-counter medications don't realize that results won't happen overnight. Their impatience drives them to shop from product to product—often making choices based on television advertising—and never really giving a product a chance to work. Finally, they give up.

If you find your mood is getting worse, that you're avoiding friends and family, or that you feel overwhelmed or hopeless, here are a few suggestions for dealing with your feelings.

Treat it. Doing something positive to control your breakouts is the best strategy for making you feel better emotionally. If you have mild acne, get to the drugstore and buy some medication. If your case looks worse than mild, make an appointment with a doctor right away.

Be patient. This is hard for teens, really hard—especially with so much pressure from your peers to look perfect. But you need to have faith that your medications will work, and you need to give them time to do their job. There's nothing like seeing your skin clear up to turn your mood around.

Find peer support. A quick search on the Internet will turn up many acne support groups with blogs, message boards, and chat rooms for teens who are going through the trials of acne. It can help to know that other kids are going through the same emotions.

Talk it out. This is where having a caring, knowledgeable doctor can pay off in ways you never expected. If you're feeling down and low, don't be afraid to mention that to your family doctor or dermatologist. Your doctor will understand. He or she has taken care of many teens facing the same frustration, anger, and depression that you may be experiencing.

Get help. If you find yourself doing self-destructive things like cutting yourself, or if your mind begins drifts toward thoughts of hurting

---

What Can I Do about Pitting and Scarring?

The first step in dealing with acne scars is to figure out which are temporary skin changes and which are permanent scars. Acne can leave flat red, white, or brown spots that will go away by themselves after a few months. Scarring is a change in the skin's texture and is more permanent. There are many treatments available, including surgery, resurfacing your skin with a laser, and smoothing out the surface by injecting it with skin fillers. Which is best for you will depend upon the type of scarring you have—puncture-like marks, round or oval depressions with sharp edges, or a rolling, wavy skin surface. You can make a decision with a dermatologist or plastic surgeon as to which technique will work best for your situation. You should know beforehand that using several approaches is necessary sometimes, and often, people need to return for several treatments. Also make certain that you look at before-and-after pictures of other patients before going ahead with any scar treatments, so that you have a better idea of what to expect.

---

yourself or ending your life, tell an adult whom you trust—a parent, a counselor, a teacher, a clergyperson, your doctor—and do it right away. Don't wait for your mood to get worse or to get better on its own.

A FINAL WORD

Acne can be unpleasant, frustrating, and depressing, but remember: For most teens, it's temporary. Although some people carry the condition into adulthood, there are many effective treatments available. Even if you're coping with a severe case, you can control the situation and avoid scarring by working closely with an understanding doctor and sticking closely to a treatment plan.

So if the mirror has been bringing you bad news lately, hang in there. With a little patience and work, it will give you a much brighter picture before you know it.

WHAT YOU NEED TO KNOW

➤ Acne results from hormonal changes in the body, not poor personal hygiene.

➤ Fried foods, fat, and sugar do not cause acne.

➤ Acne starts with skin pores plugged with sebum and dead skin cells. These plugged pores are called comedones. Closed comedones appear as whiteheads. Open comedones—those that reach the surface—are called blackheads.

➤ Overwashing can actually make acne worse. So can squeezing pimples.

➤ Wearing thick makeup can make acne worse.

➤ Some medicines and drugs, such as steroids, can cause acne flares.

➤ Acne occurs in various grades of severity, from mild (comedones only), to mild/moderate (comedones and a few papules and pustules), to moderate (many papules, pustules, and comedones), to severe (papules, pustules, cysts, and scarring).

➤ Mild acne can be treated with over-the-counter medications.

➤ Moderate to severe acne is often treated by a family physician or dermatologist.

➤ Medical treatments may include topical retinoids and benzoyl peroxide, antibiotics (both topical and systemic), and oral contraceptives.

➤ Isotretinoin is the most powerful anti-acne medication, but side effects, including birth defects in children born to mothers using the drug, make it the choice only for teens with severe acne.

➤ Anyone using isotretinoin must join and follow the iPLEDGE program, which has rules intended to prevent birth defects due to the drug.

➤ Acne is a relatively common cause of depression among teens. If you or your parents notice your mood worsening, you should bring it up with your doctor right away.

3 ▌ ▌ ▌

The Sun and Your Skin

At 16, there is no place in the world that Kristen would rather be than lying on a big, plush towel and soaking up the rays at the beach. She loves everything about it—the muffled thunder of the crashing surf, the salty smell in the air, conversation with her friends, and most of all, that hot, baking feeling that makes her so pleasantly drowsy and leaves her skin looking golden and healthy.

She likes people-watching too. There are always little kids with buckets and shovels digging in the wet sand; boys roughhousing in the water and showing off on boogie boards; elderly men on the nearby jetties casting for fish. But today, one person in particular catches her eye. It's a mom, wearing a sky-blue bandeau, a dark-red head scarf, and heart-shaped, oversized sunglasses. She has a deep, dark tan, as if she spends every summer's day in the sun. She is minding a set of twin boys, perhaps seven or eight years old, so she is probably in her thirties—but what really strikes Kristen is how much older than that the woman appears. In fact, her skin looks lined and dry, and the tan is reminiscent of antique furniture stain.

Kristen shakes her head. Women of that age, she thinks to herself, should stay out of the sun. A tan might look great when you're young, but when you get older—well, it just doesn't work. She makes a silent promise to herself that when she gets older, she will always sit under an umbrella at the beach. She doesn't want to end up looking like that mom!

Kristen's instincts about tanning are exactly right. It can make you look much older than your years, and you don't suddenly look younger again when the tan fades. Her sense of timing, however, is exactly wrong. Although that mom is certainly not helping her situation by continuing to expose herself to the midday sun, much of the damage to her skin started a long time ago—when she was Kristen's age.

GOOD OLD MR. SUN

The Sun supports life, keeps you warm, and gives you a gorgeous tan. One day, it may even become a major source of energy for running your car and heating your home. But where your skin is concerned, the Sun is not your friend. In fact, it's double trouble, because its damaging rays come in two varieties.

If you have ever seen a rainbow, which is simply white light separating into all of its parts as it passes through tiny water droplets, you have some idea of all the colors present in the Sun's rays. Some of those rays, called ultraviolet (UV), reach Earth in two wavelengths, A and B. *UVA* rays are longer than *UVBs*. (There are also UVCs, which are very short, but they don't make it through Earth's atmosphere.)

Does wavelength make a difference where your skin is concerned? Yes and no: yes in that each type of UV ray affects your skin a little differently, but no in that both types can hurt you.

That may be different from what you have heard from your friends. Many teens believe that only UVB rays are dangerous. Doctors used to believe that as well, but now we know better. It's true that UVBs can give you blistering sunburns, especially if your skin is on the pale side, while UVAs do not. And as we'll see later, UVBs also play a role in developing all of the major varieties of skin cancer.

Skin Facts: Did You Know?

People who get more regular sunlight exposure on one side of their face than the other, such as truck drivers and teachers who stand near a window, actually age much faster on that side.

UVAs, on the other hand, have enjoyed a different reputation. In fact, people perceive them as beneficial. It is this type of ray that gives you the coppery tan that makes your skin look so "healthy." And while UVB rays can cook the upper layer of your skin to blisters, UVAs go deeper under the surface without actually burning you. So what could be bad about them?

TANNING: A REALITY CHECK

No matter how great a tan may look, there is nothing healthful about it. In fact, it's a symptom of damage. When UVA rays injure your skin, cells called *melanocytes* start spitting out *melanin,* a dark, somewhat protective pigment. So just like swelling or a bruise, tanning is a signal from your skin that it has been harmed.

What kind of harm? UVAs wreak their havoc in a number of ways. First, they cause unhealthful genetic changes in your skin cells, which can lead to cancer. Most of these cancers won't fully develop until you're older, so you may not pay a price for exposure to the Sun until you're well into adulthood. However, one type—the most dangerous, unfortunately—does occur in teens. In fact, more kids than ever before are developing *melanoma* skin cancer, and doctors suspect that exposure to UVA radiation may be one of the culprits.

UVAs also break up fatty structures and weaken tiny blood vessels under your skin that keep it looking plump, smooth, and young. The effect is called photoaging, and obviously, it's not a good look—as Kristen saw. Exposure to UVA rays left that mom with wrinkled, freckled, blotchy, spider-veined skin that had a texture like leather.

You might think that this is an extreme or unusual case. It isn't. Scientists estimate that up to 80 percent of the skin's aging is due to the effects of sunlight.

THINK NATURAL SKIN

Throughout history, many cultures, including our own, considered fair or pale skin a sign of beauty and aristocracy. That's probably because a lighter complexion would have been unattainable for people who had to labor in the sun every day to earn their living, while the wealthy could afford to spend much of their time indoors.

Unfortunately, the opposite is true today. A golden tan carries the message that you have leisure time away from the classroom or office to spend lying in the sun. And no one can deny that deep bronze skin might accentuate the color of your eyes and hair and can make you

The Terrible Truth about Tanning Beds

Teens sometimes go to tanning salons to get a "base tan," that is, a gradual darkening that will give them some protection from sunburn when they go to the beach. Many also believe that because tanning beds don't use UVB radiation, they're not damaging to your skin. Unfortunately, none of this has much truth in it. A study in Sweden some years ago showed that women who used a tanning bed 10 times a year were seven times more likely to develop melanoma, the deadliest form of skin cancer. And UVAs—the type of radiation used in tanning beds—have been closely linked to premature aging of the skin. As for protection from sunburn—well, a tan has an SPF of about 4. Although it may hide the redness of a burn, it just isn't very good at protecting the skin cells from damage.

If you really want to have a tan but don't want to injure your skin in the process, a self-tanning lotion or spray-on tan is probably your best bet. There are lots of great products out there. Look for tanners that contain dihydroacetone (DHA). They will give you natural-looking color, rather than the fake orange skin color you can get with some products. One warning, however: A self-tanning lotion or air-spray tan from a salon does not protect you from the sun's UV rays. So if you're headed for the beach, a cruise, or a hike in the mountains, be sure to wear a sunscreen with at least a 30 SPF.

feel more physically attractive. As a result, a tan is now perceived as a sign of good health, while paleness is sometimes seen as an indication of sickliness or social isolation.

Obviously, avoiding a tan is a difficult choice for teens. Being your own person, making decisions about what is best for you no matter what the current fashion or trend, is doubly hard with so much peer pressure to conform to other people's standards. Many, even after they learn the facts, decide to continue browning their skin. But make no mistake: If you tan now, you will age much sooner than you ever expected to. If you doubt it, just look at the adults all around you. Many of them grew up at a time when the dangers of sun exposure

---

Skin Facts: Did You Know?

Protection against solar radiation is as important in the winter as it is in the summer, especially if the light is reflecting off of ice or snow.

---

weren't well known. The consequences are written all over their faces.

As hard a choice as it may be for some, going for "fair and natural" rather than "golden and bronzed" now will pay off for years to come. (And just imagine how jealous your friends will be when you end up looking 10 or 15 years younger than they do.)

ON ANOTHER WAVELENGTH

The deep injuries that UVAs leave behind are, of course, only part of the picture. UVBs wreak their own kind of havoc closer to the surface of your skin.

First of all, they cause sunburn. The deep, painful redness that can appear after a day at the beach is actually an inflammatory reaction to UVB radiation exposure. At its worst, sunburn can cause swelling and blistering, as if you had actually been scorched by a flame. As the redness begins to fade, of course, your skin peels and flakes off—and for good reason.

UVB radiation burns are not the same as simple scalds or heat burns. They affect your cells at a genetic level, causing the *DNA* in your cells to change in self-destructive ways. These changes can lead to cancer. In fact, recent research shows that UVB rays are even more likely than UVA rays to have this effect because the changes they cause are more difficult for the body to repair. When you get a sunburn, the cellular damage may be so great that your immune system simply signals the cells to commit suicide. This process is called *apoptosis*. As the cells die, you get rid of them like a snake shedding its skin.

Unfortunately, not all damaged cells go away. And perhaps even more importantly, UVB rays can actually cripple the repair mechanisms—the immune system cells—that exist in lower layers of skin, so that over time, the skin repair process doesn't work so well. The damage, as with UVA radiation, accumulates. Your skin gradually builds up a backload of damaged cells, significantly raising your risk for premature aging and cancer.

Finally, you have probably noticed that some people burn more easily than others. Those with darker complexions enjoy a certain amount of natural protection from the sun, in the form of extra melanin in their skin. However, everyone, no matter how dark your skin, will eventually burn from too much sun exposure, and UVB radiation can actually cause damage without giving you any noticeable inflammation. That means that everyone, *everyone*, needs to protect himself or herself.

GOOD SUN SENSE

For the sake of argument, let us suppose that you do decide to avoid tanning. Does that mean you have to hide away in a cave for the rest of your life? Of course not. You're not a bat or a vampire. You can, however, manage your sun exposure so that you don't end up with symptoms of skin damage: a burn, tan, or mass of freckles. Basically, it comes down to using three simple sun-protection tools: timing, clothing, and screening.

Timing. When the sun is high in the sky, its rays are more intense than when it sits low on the horizon, so it makes sense to avoid exposure during these peak hours. Generally, that means staying mostly

What about the "Sunshine Vitamin?"

Lately, there has been some controversy around the role of sunshine and getting enough vitamin D into your system. In fact, UV rays do stimulate skin cells to produce this vitamin, which is necessary for good health. However, there are safer ways than baking in the midday sun to get adequate amounts. The first, obviously, is to take a vitamin D supplement. The recommended daily intake for teens, set by the National Institutes of Health, is 200 IU a day. Fatty fish such as tuna, salmon, and mackerel are good dietary sources of vitamin D.

indoors or in the shade between the hours of 10:00 A.M. to 3:00 P.M. during the summer months (daylight savings time) and 11:00 A.M. to 4:00 P.M. during the winter and early spring (standard time). This is a great time to wander around the mall, take a nap, watch some television, or sit under a beach umbrella.

The UV index is another tool you can use to time your forays into the sunlight. Basically, it is a number, assigned by the U.S. Environmental Protection Agency's SunWise Program every day, that indicates the risk of overexposure to UV rays on that day in a particular zip code. Here's what the numbers on the index mean:

UV INDEX	
UV Index Number	**Exposure Level**
2 or less	Low
3 to 5	Moderate
6 to 8	High
8 to 10	Very High
11+	Extreme

A UV alert is a warning the EPA gives when the intensity of the Sun's radiation is expected to be unusually high on a given day. You can find the UV index and UV alerts at the EPA's SunWise Web site: www. epa.gov/sunwise/uvindex.html.

Clothing. Dressing for the sun can be tricky. On one hand, you want to choose clothing that helps protect you from UV exposure. On the other, you don't want to end up looking geeky. Possible? Of course. Clothing is just one part of an overall sun-sense strategy. It's not supposed to do the whole job, so you don't have to bundle up like a mummy to get positive benefits. With a little thought and care, you can dress in a way that makes you look good and helps preserve your complexion at the same time.

To keep your upper body from harmful UV radiation, wear rash guard or SPF-rated shirts. Some of these products block up to 97 percent of the Sun's rays. You can find them at your favorite retail stores at the beginning of the beach season, and generally any surf shop will carry them all through the summer. Wearing either a full-length or three-quarter length tee shirt can also be helpful. For any garment to screen radiation successfully, it should have a tight weave, so there is no place for the Sun's rays to get through.

The SunWise Program

The SunWise Program is a national environmental and health education program, administered by the Environmental Protection Agency, aimed at teaching people how to protect themselves from overexposure to the sun. It partners with schools, communities, and nonprofit programs to deliver its message. The SunWise Web site (www.epa.gov/SunWise) contains a wealth of information about solar radiation and its effects on health, as well as about how ozone depletion of the atmosphere has increased the general risk for skin cancers.

Cover your head. Wearing a hat in the sun is always a good idea, but selecting the right kind of hat is important. A baseball cap, for example, will cover your forehead, but it won't do anything for your ears or the back of your neck in bright sunlight. Something more like a floppy surf hat, which protects the entire face, ears, and neck, is a better choice.

Shade your eyes. Most teens wear sunglasses when at the beach or pool, which is a very good idea. Over the long term, UV exposure can cause your eyes to form *cataracts,* a clouding of the lenses that interferes with vision and can only be repaired with surgery. Even more seriously, melanoma—the most serious form of sun-related skin cancer—can form in the eyes. Selecting sunglasses that offer you maximum protection, however, is important. Don't make the mistake of assuming that a high price tag indicates high-quality lenses. Whatever your budget, look for a pair that offers 99- to 100-percent UV protection. The tint should be dark enough to keep the glare down, but not so dark that you can't clearly see the shapes and colors around you. Finally, remember that sunlight can still enter from the sides of many glasses and reflect into your eyes, so consider wearing wrap-around lenses.

Sunscreen. Wearing sunscreen is the only concession many teens are willing to make when it comes to defending against solar radiation. Unfortunately, that's like leaving your helmet at home and expecting knee pads to give you all the protection you need when

Sun Poisoning: An Allergy to the Sun?

Sun poisoning, known medically as polymorphous light eruption, is a rash that some people develop after exposure to UV radiation. It can be red, bumpy, itchy, burning, or blistering, and tends to appear mostly on the front of the neck, chest, and thighs—although it can affect any area of your skin. In the worst cases, it can also make you feel sick with fever, nausea, and vomiting. To call sun poisoning an "allergic reaction" may be a stretch, but like an allergy, it is an inflammatory response that only a few people have. We know that it results from a particularly high sensitivity to UV rays, but beyond that, no one knows why the condition occurs. Sun poisoning will usually go away on its own after a few days. If you have this kind of sensitivity to sunlight, you need to protect yourself. That means staying out of the sun, especially at peak times; wearing protective clothing; and slathering yourself with sunblock, which stops all UV rays from getting through. It goes without saying that you should steer clear of tanning salons.

you're rollerblading. You should use a sunscreen in combination with timing and clothing to achieve the best results. But if applying lotion is the only protection you want, it still pays to do it right. This means selecting a product that is strong enough, applying it properly, and reapplying it appropriately. Here are some tips:

> **Remember, sunscreen is not sunblock.** Sunscreen and sunblock are not the same thing. Sunblocks contain minerals, usually titanium oxide or zinc oxide, that keep all UV radiation from reaching your skin. These formulations used to be heavy and thick, but recently many new, lighter versions have become available. If you have sensitive skin or eczema, a sunblock will be less irritating.
> **Go for full protection.** To get the most protection from your sunscreen, choose one that is labeled "broad spectrum." This means that it will defend against both UVA and UVB rays. A high sun protection factor (SPF) does *not* mean a product

defends against both types of UV radiation. SPF applies only to UVBs.

> **Consider the dampness factor.** If you're sweating or swimming, choose a product that is water-resistant or waterproof and reapply it often.
> **Select a product your skin will like.** For skin that is sensitive or prone to acne, noncomedogenic sunscreens are available.
> **Check the SPF.** You should choose a product with a high SPF, preferably 30 or more, but be aware that a 30 SPF does not mean that the product filters out twice as much radiation as one with a 15 SPF. It simply means that if you're not sweating hard or swimming, you should be able to spend twice as long in the sun without burning.
> **Lay it on thick and often.** Apply sunscreen 20 to 30 minutes before going out, then reapply it every couple of hours—more often than that if you're splashing around in the water or sweating profusely. On average, you should use about an ounce of lotion for each full-body application.
> **Check the expiration date.** Sunscreens usually expire after about a year. Check the date on yours and make certain it is current.

Will Wearing a Sunscreen Make Acne Worse?

Sunscreens, like any other cream or lotion you put on your face, can aggravate acne, but if you're careful about what you use, you can minimize or eliminate the problem. Look for products that are oil free and labeled noncomedogenic. Also, take the time to find a sunscreen you feel comfortable with. Some have a greasy texture that you might not care for, or a scent that might bother you. Find a product that you can wear comfortably every day, even during the winter. By the way, although it is true that some sun exposure can be beneficial in calming an acne flare-up, generally speaking, the benefits don't outweigh the damage the radiation will cause to your skin.

Finally, it is always a good idea to keep well hydrated, both while you are in the sun and afterward. Drink plenty of water, and use a moisturizing lotion to prevent dryness.

TREATING SUNBURN

Sunburn can be a painful reminder that you have had too much UVB exposure. It is always best, of course, to avoid burning in the first place, but once you've turned lobster red, there are still some things you can do relieve the discomfort.

First, use ibuprofen for pain. It is both an *analgesic* (painkiller) and anti-inflammatory medication, so it helps calm sunburn symptoms in two ways. However, it will *not* reverse the damage that has been done to your cells.

If the sunburn is mild, use a moisturizer. A lot of people apply aloe, but that is not really necessary. Usually a thick moisturizing cream or ointment will do the trick. Using cool compresses or soaking in a cool bath can also help.

For more severe, blistering sunburns, take ibuprofen more frequently, and call your doctor. He or she can prescribe a mid-to-high potency topical corticosteroid that will provide some relief.

CANCER

No one likes to think about the possibility of getting cancer, but for teens, there are good reasons to become vigilant about it. For one, you can significantly lower your risk of future disease by protecting

Skin Facts: Did You Know?

Although they're sometimes confused, freckles and moles are not the same thing. Freckles are areas of increased pigment that the skin has released in response to the sun. They may fade with less sun exposure. They do not turn into skin cancer. A mole, also called a *nevus*, is a collection of melanocytes, cells that produce pigment. Moles are permanent and do carry a risk of becoming cancerous.

yourself from the sun today. UV radiation damage is cumulative—the more you accumulate, the higher your risk for skin tumors. If you cut back your sun exposure now and avoid tanning beds like the plague, you will be less likely to end up with this kind of problem 10 or 20 years from now.

The other reason is more immediate. Although there are many different types of skin cancer, the three most common are all associated with UV damage to the skin. Two of them can take years to decades to develop and rarely show up in teens. The third is a type that teens can and do develop, and knowing its warning signs can save your life.

Basal cell carcinoma (BCC). This type of tumor occurs in cells that line the lowest part of the outer skin, the epidermis, and most are due to overexposure to the sun. Although they are still relatively rare among teens, the average age for the appearance of BCC has been getting lower every year. They are the most common cancer people get—about one in five individuals will develop a basal cell carcinoma in his or her lifetime. Close to a million new cases occur each year. Although they often appear as a smooth, pearly, or waxy bumps on the face, ears, neck, scalp, shoulders, and back, they can also show up on the trunk or arms and legs as flat lesions that are colored pink, red, or brown. Occasionally, this cancer will look scaly—more like a patch of psoriasis or eczema. These cancers rarely metastasize, that is, spread to parts of the body beyond the original site, but they do grow in size and can extend to the deep tissues below the surface of the skin. Removal of a BCC needs to be complete and leaves scarring. Removing an advanced BCC can leave you noticeably, even severely, disfigured.

Squamous cell carcinoma (SCC). This is the second most common cancer, and it occurs in flat cells, called squamous cells, on the skin's surface. About a quarter of a million new cases are diagnosed each year. SCCs can develop anywhere on the body, but they usually show up on sun-exposed areas such as the scalp, neck, face, ears, lips, arms, hands, and legs. An SCC may appear as a hard, red bump that looks almost like a pimple, or as a scaly, flat lesion. It can itch, bleed, and become crusty. Although these tumors can take a long time to spread, they can advance beyond their original site if not completely removed. This, unfortunately, can lead to death. SCC almost never occurs among teens and are most common in people over age 50. However, as mentioned above, the cellular changes that lead to these tumors can start when you're young.

Skin Facts: Did You Know?

You can get sunburn on your lips as easily as anywhere else on your body! And skin cancers can develop on them. Whenever you're out in the sunlight, wear a lip balm with at least a 15 SPF. Don't depend upon lipstick or gloss to give the protection—they won't. Your best bet is to put on a layer of balm before applying any makeup to your lips.

Melanoma. Melanoma is the rarest of the three UV-related cancers, and the deadliest. Currently, about 8,500 people die in the United States every year from this disease. And this is the one that teens must be most wary of, particularly if you have a parent, sibling or grandparent with this type of skin cancer. Fortunately, melanoma can often be spotted early in its growth cycle and be removed before it becomes an irreversible problem. In fact, if caught early, it is almost 100 percent curable. Once it has spread beyond its original site to other organs, however, it is very difficult to treat.

So it is important to know what to look for. Melanoma can closely resemble a normal mole, although upon closer inspection, it may actually look a little odd—more like a mole gone wrong. It can develop in an existing nevus or appear as a new one. Although melanoma is linked to UV exposure, it can occur in the mouth or internal organs.

Here are ABCDEs of melanoma—the warning the signs to look for:

> **Asymmetry.** This means that if you drew a line through the center of the mole, the two sides would not match in shape. It does not follow the silhouette of a regular circle or oval.
> **Border.** This means that the edges of the mole are not smooth or even. They may be notched or scalloped, or most importantly, they may seem to fade into the normal surrounding skin.
> **Color.** Look for unusual, brilliant colors like blue-black or coffee brown. Even more telling are moles that contain more than one color. These can include: brown, black, tan, white, red, blue, or others.
> **Diameter.** These moles are often 6mm across or larger. That's about the size of a pencil eraser. However, this test does not

The Self-Exam

A regular self-exam is an important tool in spotting skin cancers early, when they're highly curable. Here's what to do:

➤ Look over your head, face, and neck, using mirrors for difficult or impossible-to-see areas. Using the cool air of a blow dryer to part your hair, thoroughly examine your scalp.

➤ Check both the palms and backs of your hands. Likewise, check your nails—melanomas can grow under them. Check the fronts and backs of your arms, your elbows, and your underarms.

➤ Examine your chest and abdominal areas. Women should check under their breasts as well.

➤ Using a bathroom or full-length mirror and a hand mirror, check your back from shoulders to heels.

➤ Check your genitals and the area between your legs with a hand mirror.

➤ Sit down and carefully inspect your feet, including the soles, between the toes, and under the nails.

apply to moles you were born with, which are often larger than that.

➤ **Evolving.** Any change in a black or brown spot can signal danger. This includes any alteration in size, shape, elevation, or color. Also be on the lookout for pain, itching, bleeding, or crusting.

Any spot on your body that exhibits any of these symptoms is your signal to get to a doctor. Don't wait weeks or months. It's not an emergency room situation, but don't procrastinate. Even a doctor who normally makes appointments months in advance will make room for you in his or her schedule if you have an unusual or changing mole.

The Ugly Duckling

Although the ABCDEs of identifying a melanoma will catch many of these cancers, not every bad mole will fall into any of the five categories. Because of this, some doctors have added a sixth category, which they call the "Ugly duckling." Basically, the idea is to look for moles that stand out from all the other black and brown spots around them. If there is one nevus that is bigger, darker, or of a different shape or color than others nearby, it is a signal to have a doctor take a look at it.

YOUR RISK

Although anyone of any color or shade can develop skin cancers, certain skin types are more vulnerable than others. Even people with skin types that do not easily or ever burn are at risk for skin cancer and the damaging effects of the sun. Sun protection is still advisable. The following table can help you determine your skin type:

 I. You always burn and never tan.
 II. You almost always burn and rarely tan.
 III. You sometimes burn and sometimes tan.
 IV. You tend to tan easily and are less likely to burn.
 V. You tan easily and rarely burn.
 VI. You never burn and have dark skin.

Skin types I and II have the highest risk for UV-related skin cancers. Other factors that raise your risk for melanoma skin cancer include:

> Having a close relative—mother, father, sibling—who has had melanoma.
> Having many dysplastic (unusual) moles on your skin or having a close relative with many dysplastic moles. Dysplastic moles may look somewhat like a normal mole, but they may be larger and also have similarities to the appearance of melanoma.
> Excessive ultraviolet sun exposure (including tanning beds).
> Having had a melanoma in the past.

SKIN CANCER TREATMENT

How your doctor treats your skin cancer will depend upon its type and location. For basal and squamous cell carcinomas, he or she will most likely surgically remove the visible tumor and some area around it to catch any hidden cancerous cells there. The removed tissue will then go to a medical specialist called a *pathologist,* who will examine it microscopically, identify any malignancy, and indicate whether enough surgery had been done to completely get rid of the cancer.

If the lesion comes back, or if it is located in an area, such as the nose, where a larger scar would be disfiguring, a technique called *Mohs microscopic surgery* is the treatment of choice. In Mohs, the doctor removes only the cancerous cells by slicing away the tumor one layer at a time and examining each sample under a microscope. When the doctor reaches a layer that is completely cancer free, the surgery is over.

For melanoma, the treatment will also begin by surgically removing the tumor and a fair amount of skin from the surrounding area. How much will depend on how large and thick the visible tumor is. A pathologist will examine the tissue to determine if more surgery is needed. In the case of melanoma, further surgery is often necessary. It is important to remove all cancerous cells completely with a wide margin to spare. Sometimes, skin repair with surgical techniques called *grafts* or flaps are necessary to complete the operation.

If the melanoma skin cancer is deep and thick, it may also be necessary to remove and test local *lymph nodes* for the spread of the melanoma cells. These nodes are little bean-shaped organs, located throughout the body, that can capture bacteria and cancer cells.

For tumors that are more advanced and have spread to other organs, treatments may include *chemotherapy* (taking drugs that kill cancer cells), immunotherapy (taking drugs that trigger your immune system to kill cancer cells), and/or *radiation therapy* (using X-rays or other forms of radiation to kill cancer cells).

A FINAL WORD

Although your skin may have already accumulated some UV damage, it is never too late to change course and head in a more healthful direction. By timing your exposure, wearing proper clothing, and appropriately using sunscreen, you can slow down the aging process, avoid painful sunburns, and significantly lower your risk for skin cancers. Again, this might not be an easy choice to make. It might require you to miss spending time with friends who remain unconvinced about

Self-Exam Checklist

The six warning signs of melanoma:

Asymmetrical. One half doesn't look like the other half.

Borders. The edges are irregular or poorly defined.

Color. Varied color from one area to another.

Diameter. The size of a pencil eraser or bigger.

Evolving. Any change in size, color, or shape.

Doesn't match. Any mole that looks different from those that surround it.

the dangers of UV radiation. And if you really want that bronzed look, you will need to spend some time applying a self-tanning product or getting a spray tan at a salon. But in the end, when you look in the mirror, you'll have proof positive that the choice you made was the right one.

WHAT YOU NEED TO KNOW

➤ Both types of ultraviolet (UV) rays, UVA and UVB, cause damage to your skin. Combined, they can cause premature aging and skin cancer.

➤ A tan is the skin's way of trying to protect itself from further damage, but a tan only appears after some damage has already been done.

➤ Avoid going out in the sun between the hours of 10:00 A.M. and 3:00 P.M. during the summer. Adjust those times an hour forward in the winter.

➤ Wear tightly woven clothing, such as SPF-rated tee shirts, in the sun. Avoid fabrics that allow sunlight through.

➤ Apply a full spectrum sunscreen with a 30 or higher SPF 20 to 30 minutes before going out. Reapply once an hour unless you're sweating or swimming. Then apply more often.

▸ Checking the UV index before going out will give you a good idea of the Sun's intensity on any given day.

▸ For mild sunburns, take ibuprofen and apply a moisturizer. A cool bath can also help.

▸ For severe, blistering sunburns, call your doctor.

▸ There are three common types of skin cancer related to UV exposure. Two of them, basal cell and squamous cell carcinoma, are rare in teens. The most deadly kind, melanoma, does occur among teens.

▸ Melanomas can arise from existing moles or appear as new ones. Any mole that has unusual coloring, size, or shape is a signal to see a doctor as is any mole that changes in any way or appears different from surrounding moles. Do a self-exam once a month, and get a yearly exam from your doctor—especially if you have a family history of melanoma, or if you are fair skinned, have red or blond hair, or green or blue eyes.

4 ||

Cuts, Burns, and Other Things That Hurt

Fifteen-year-old Justin was walking the family dog, a golden retriever named Henry, when it happened. It was dusk, and a light rain had begun to fall. As boy and dog made their way down a neighborhood street, something caught Henry's attention, maybe a rabbit or a squirrel, because he suddenly stopped short, his ears perked up, and his eyes fixed on a particular spot in the dark. Justin barely noticed. He hunched his shoulders and adjusted his jacket's collar for a little protection from the cold drizzle. Then, so quickly that there was no time to react, Henry shot forward after the invisible prey. Justin scrambled to keep his balance on the damp pavement while trying to rein in the dog. Too late. His feet were already out from under him. He tumbled backward, landing hard on his left forearm, which he had automatically thrust behind him to break his fall.

When he got back to his feet, his arm was bleeding profusely. Henry sat and gave him a curious look. Justin could barely make out the wound for all the blood. It didn't look too serious, but how was he to know for sure? Mom and Dad had gone out for the evening. Should he just rinse it off and apply bandages? Or did he need stitches? He hated the idea of dialing 911. He didn't want to make a big deal out of nothing. There were friends he could call to drive him to the ER, but on a Saturday night, kids with cars weren't at home waiting to hear from friends with problems. Why did this have to happen now?

UNPLEASANT SURPRISES

No doubt about it, there are times when knowing something about first aid can come in handy. Accidents happen, and rarely do they happen at a convenient time. It pays to be ready and prepared. When these mishaps involve the skin, getting appropriate treatment quickly is important, because some injuries can leave disfiguring scars or lead to serious infections. But as Justin found out, knowing what constitutes "appropriate" may not be so obvious. Fortunately, a little knowledge can go a long way where skin wounds are concerned. Below are some tips for treating some of the more common ones.

ABRASIONS, CUTS, AND PUNCTURES

Falling is among the most frequent causes of wounds among young people, and a minor *abrasion*—a scrape, rug burn, or "road rash" on the skin over a bony surface such as an elbow or knee—is undoubtedly the most common type. Usually, abrasions aren't cause for alarm, but they are unsightly and can be very painful, especially as they become inflamed a day or two after they first occur.

Providing that the entire depth of the skin has not been damaged (a full-thickness or *avulsion* injury), you can usually treat an abrasion

Avulsions and Skin Flaps

If a scrape has completely torn away the skin down to the fat, muscle, or bone, the wound is called an avulsion. If the torn-off skin remains attached on one side, it is called a flap. To treat an avulsion, clean around the wound carefully, removing any debris; apply antibiotic ointment, and dress it with a bandage. Then get to a medical professional as soon as possible. Avulsions larger than an inch in diameter may require a skin graft. If there is a flap, clean the wound, and then carefully lay the flap back over it. When you bandage it, don't seal the bandage tightly all around. Leave spaces to allow for drainage. Again, get to a doctor or nurse as soon as possible for treatment.

without seeing a medical professional such as a doctor or nurse. The same is true for minor cuts. The question, of course, is what does "minor" mean?

If a cut is shallow; doesn't gape open; doesn't obviously go below the bottom layer of skin to bone, fat, or muscle; and isn't located on your face (where it may need professional treatment to keep it from becoming disfiguring), self-treatment is probably okay. Here is how to treat either an abrasion or minor cut.

Stop the bleeding. Apply pressure to the wound. If you use your bare hand, make sure to wash it first so you don't transmit bacteria to the injury. If you're treating someone else's wound, wear rubber gloves or put several layers of clean cloth between your hand and the wound so that you're not exposed to any blood-borne diseases the person may have. Apply constant pressure for fifteen minutes. Except for minor oozing, if the bleeding hasn't stopped, see a medical professional.

Clean the wound. Using mild soap and water, gently wash out remaining debris and dirt from the cut or scrape. This will help remove any bacteria that could develop into an infection. If you suspect any debris, such as glass particles, remains in the wound, see a physician or nurse. Do not use concentrated hydrogen peroxide or alcohol, as these can actually slow healing.

Use an antibiotic ointment. Applying an ointment containing bacitracin, neomycin, or polymyxin B can help reduce the risk of infection, and it can help keep the wound moist. The old-school idea was to let a wound dry out and develop a scab, but current thought is to keep the injury wet and covered to reduce the possibility of scarring and to speed healing. Obviously, if you know you have an allergy to any of these antibiotics, don't use it.

Apply a bandage. Smaller cuts and scrapes can heal without a bandage, but applying one can further protect you against infection and help keep the wound moist to help prevent scarring. Bandages should be nonstick—that is, they should have a surface that won't stick to the wound so that when you remove it, you won't pull off newly healed skin cells. Avoid gauze pads, as they have loose fibers that cause pain when they are removed from the wound. Bandages can either be self-adhesive or affixed with tape. For people who have very sensitive skin, paper tape might be the best option.

Let it heal. Change the dressing once or twice a day until the wound is completely healed. You will know it's healed when the area is smooth and without any depression or remaining scab. If you notice any swelling, redness, itching, or pus at the injury sight while it is healing, see a medical professional.

Puncture wounds, which can be caused by anything from a safety pin to a ball point pen to a nail, represent a special case. Because they are difficult to clean and closing them with stitches or staples may increase the chance of infection, oftentimes puncture wounds are left untreated. However, it is probably a good idea to have a medical professional make treatment decisions about punctures rather than trying to determine that yourself.

BRUISES

A bruise, known medically as a *contusion,* occurs when an injury causes tiny blood vessels to break and bleed into the skin. Usually, a

Is a Tetanus Shot Necessary?

One worrisome condition that can develop from a wound is called tetanus, which can lead to death. *Tetanus* results from poisons, produced by the *Clostridium tetani* bacteria, that affect the central nervous system. The bacteria grow in soil everywhere in the world, and—although this is rare—they can enter the body through any open wound, including insect and animal bites and splinters. As the bacteria's toxins take effect, they send muscles into violent spasms, which eventually become one continuous, paralyzing spasm. As the muscles in the face, head, and neck freeze up, the victim can no longer open his or her mouth, which is why tetanus has been nicknamed "lockjaw." While there are treatments that can work after the infection has started, prevention is the best policy. Presuming that you had your first series of tetanus vaccinations before you were five, you should get a booster every 10 years thereafter. If you sustain a deep wound during that time, your doctor may decide to give you a booster early, and your next one would be due 10 years from that date.

Skin Facts: Did You Know?

You can get a bruise anywhere, even under a nail! As with every medical condition, doctors have their own word for this: subungual hematoma. Pressure from the gathering blood can make these injuries pretty painful, but they're simple to treat. Apply cold compresses for 24 hours. If the bruise continues to expand or becomes too painful, your doctor can relieve the pressure by burning a hole through the nail. This does not hurt, because the nail is made of dead cells, and you will get instant relief.

bruise will begin as a tender, raised, blue-black area. Those that are more flat and purplish are called *ecchymoses*. Tiny pinpoints of red or purple under the skin—miniature bruises—are called *petechiae*. Bruises are often painful, and when deep, can cause weakness in nearby muscles. Applying a cold compress is usually the best treatment. Bruises can take weeks to fade away, and they go through various stages of color—purple to green and brown—before they disappear entirely.

You may have noticed that some people bruise more easily than others. That can happen for many reasons—an inherited genetic trait, advancing age (this applies to older adults with thinner skin), and bleeding disorders. Some medications that thin the blood, such as aspirin, can also make you bruise more easily. So can corticosteroids, such as prednisone, which make the skin thinner, and nutritional supplements, including fish oil, ginkgo, ginger, and garlic.

If you notice unexplained ecchymoses or petechiae in more than one area of skin, let your doctor know. Rarely, these can be symptoms of a more serious condition.

ANIMAL BITES

Most animal bites happen with pets, and they can put you at significant risk for infection. Dogs cause the most bites, but cats cause the most infections. You can treat minor bites, where the skin is either barely or not broken, as you would any minor wound. Stop the bleeding, clean it, apply antibiotic ointment, and bandage it. If you're not up-to-date with your tetanus boosters, get one immediately. Check the bite mark frequently for signs of infection—redness, swelling, or pus—and if any appear, see a doctor.

Deep punctures, skin tears, or gaping wounds require immediate medical care. Go to an emergency room. Again, make sure you get a tetanus booster if you need one. The ER doctor may also treat you with an oral antibiotic.

Wild animal bites (and scratches) carry an additional risk: *rabies.* Rabies is an extremely serious disease, caused by a virus, that affects the nerves and brain. If not treated quickly, it will lead to death. So it's important to seek immediate treatment for the bite or scratch of any wild animal or any pet that may have been exposed to any rabies-carrying animals. Wild animals that commonly carry rabies include bats, foxes, coyotes, raccoons, and skunks. Squirrels and other rodents rarely carry the disease, but you should never presume that the bite of any wild animal is rabies-free.

This is true no matter how small or insignificant the bite or scratch may appear. In the case of bats, the bite or scratch may be so small that you can't detect a mark on the skin, so any physical contact with this particular animal should be treated as a bite. Simply discovering that a bat has been in your home should also be considered a potential exposure. You may have had contact without even knowing it.

For a wild animal bite, here is what to do:

> ▸ Wash the site with soap and water for a minimum of 10 minutes.

Cold Compresses

To make a cold compress, put ice in a baggy, and then wrap it with a towel. Instead of ice, you can take a bag of frozen vegetables from the freezer or purchase reusable compresses made of soft gel from your drugstore. In any case, it's a good idea to keep some kind of compress ready in your freezer, because injuries, aches, and pains that require cold treatment are common. For most first aid treatments, apply a compress for 10 to 15 minutes every hour or two for a couple of days.

Skin Facts: Did You Know?

Any bat can carry rabies, but those that appear during the daytime, end up in places where they shouldn't be (such as a room in your home), or can't fly are the most suspicious.

> Get to a doctor, clinic, or emergency room immediately.
> Notify your local health department.
> If the animal is incapacitated, dead, or easily captured, call your local animal control to capture it and send it off for testing.

HUMAN BITES

Human bites are a nasty business, and luckily, by the time we reach our teen years, most of us don't go around sinking our teeth into each other. Sometimes, however, during sports, roughhousing, or even fights, one person's tooth can inadvertently break another person's skin. This may not seem like a bite, but for medical purposes, it is. Any time you cut your skin on another person's teeth, your system becomes exposed to all kinds of organisms, bacteria and viruses that shouldn't be there, so you need to treat the wound. In fact, the risk of infection makes human bites as potentially dangerous as animal bites. Here's what to do:

> Apply pressure to stop the bleeding.
> Clean the wound with soap and water.
> Apply antibiotic ointment.
> Put on a sterile bandage.
> See a doctor. If you're not up-to-date with your tetanus boosters, you'll need to get one within 48 hours. Your doctor may want to start you on an oral antibiotic.

SNAKEBITES

If you go camping or hiking almost anywhere in the United States—with the exception of Maine, Alaska, and Hawaii—snakebite is one of the hazards you need to be aware of. There are four species of venomous snake in this country: rattlesnakes, copperheads, cotton-mouths, and coral snakes. They break down into 20 subspecies. Some are more dangerous than others, but none are harmless. The type of poison they carry differs from species to species.

The American Red Cross recommends that every snakebite, even by a non-venomous variety, should be treated as a medical emergency. That's because it's not always easy to tell a poisonous snake from a nonpoisonous one, and bite marks are not always obvious. Coral snakes, for example, look very much like some harmless species, and they do not leave fang marks. And even a bite from a benign species like a black snake can cause an infection or allergic reaction.

Obviously, your first line of defense is to avoid these critters. Wear heavy boots if you're going to be walking in tall grass. Don't pick up firewood or large rocks if you don't know what is waiting beneath them, and keep your extremities out of dark places. Be careful where you place your hands when climbing over rocks. And if you see a snake, leave it alone. Don't try to get closer to observe it, and don't try to kill it. Some snakes can strike over half of their body length, so getting close may get you into trouble.

If you do get bitten by a snake, here is what to do:

> **Don't panic.** Most bites are not fatal, if properly cared for.
> **Wash the wound.** Use soap and water to scrub away any venom or infectious material from around the wound.
> **Do *not* elevate.** Try, if possible, to keep the wound lower than your heart. This will help slow down the circulation of the poison to other parts of the body.
> **Get help.** See a medical emergency professional as soon as possible. He or she will determine what kind of treatment you need.
> **Tie off the bite.** If you're bitten on an arm or leg, you can wrap a bandage or belt three to four inches above the wound. However, *do not* tie off the blood flow entirely. Leave enough slack in the bandage so that you can slip a finger under it.
> **Apply suction.** Snakebite kits often provide suction cups to help remove venom from the wound. This will *not* remove poison that has already reached the bloodstream or muscle tissue. Under no circumstances should you try to suck venom from the wound with your mouth.

A couple of other precautions: Don't cut into or around the wound, as doing so will only cause further damage to your skin; and don't apply ice, as cool temperatures can cause harm in this case.

Skin Facts: Did You Know?

Up to 30 percent of bites from venomous snakes contain no poison! Experts believe this is because the animals accidentally release their venom before the bite occurs.

BLISTERS

Blisters can occur from friction and burns (heat, chemical, and sun). Blisters (called vesicles when they are small) can be left intact in some cases and can be carefully popped in others. The skin over a blister helps provides a shield against infection, but sometimes the pressure of this fluid causes pain or helps the blister get bigger and spread. If a foot blister is rubbing against your shoe and causing too much pain or a hand blister is preventing you from using that hand, you can safely pop and drain it it by following these suggestions:

> ➤ Wash the blister with soap and water.
> ➤ Swab it with alcohol.
> ➤ Use a needle sterilized with a flame (make sure the metal has cooled) or washed with alcohol to puncture the side of the blister.
> ➤ Apply antibiotic ointment and a nonstick bandage to the area.
> ➤ Do not remove the roof of the blister—just gently deflate it.

To prevent friction blisters, protect any area of skin that you're likely to rub a lot. You can do that by making sure to wear shoes that fit properly, wearing gloves (if practical) when you're doing yard work or playing sports, or putting a bandage over the area to protect it.

BURNS AND SCALDS

Burns and scalds frighten everyone, and for good reason. According to the American Burn Association (www.ameriburn.org), every year these injuries send half a million people for medical treatment, 40,000 to hospitals, and 4,000 to their death. Burns can be extraordinarily painful. They are prone to infection and can also leave victims permanently disfigured.

Getting appropriate treatment is important, as it can mean the difference between a good and a poor outcome. To establish whether a burn is minor or serious, you need to determine how badly it has damaged the skin tissue. Generally, burns fall into one of three classes:

First degree. The skin is red, possibly swollen, and can be painful but is not burnt through. These injuries are usually minor, and you can treat them at home unless they cover large areas of your hands, feet, face, groin, buttocks, or major joints.

Second degree. The affected area is deep red, blistered, blotchy, swollen, and intensely painful. The top layer of skin is burned through, and the next layer, the dermis, has been scorched. If the burn is less than three inches wide and not on the hands, feet, face, groin, buttocks, or major joints, you can treat it at home. If it is larger, or if it is on any of the body areas listed, get medical help immediately.

Lip Protection

Sore, chapped lips can become so irritated that they crack and bleed—not so great for your smile. Habitual lip licking is the most common culprit. There are enzymes—proteins that encourage chemical reactions—in your saliva that actually have mild digestive properties. With repeated application over time, these enzymes eat away at the surface skin on your lips. To protect yourself, use a moisturizing cream or lip balm that has an SPF of at least 15 regularly, and stop licking your lips!

Another common condition in the same area is called angular cheilitis or angular stomatitis, but both names are just a fancy way of saying cracks in the corners of your mouth. This often happens as a result of irritation from saliva combined with an overgrowth of yeast—a fungus that naturally occurs in the mouth. You can treat it by mixing a little hydrocortisone 1% cream with an over-the-counter antifungal cream and applying it to the affected area.

Third degree. The affected area is burned all the way through the skin to the fat, muscle, or even bone beneath. There may be no pain in this type of burn, as the nerves that relay pain signals to your brain can be destroyed. Skin involved in the burn may appear charred black or dry and white.

Going into Shock

Severe cuts, wounds, and burns can cause you to go into a state of shock, which basically means that changes in blood flow cause your body to shut down. Left untreated, shock can be deadly. Here is a checklist of symptoms to be aware of:

Confusion, restlessness, or irritability

Feeling faint or dizzy

Nausea

Pallor/unusually pale skin

Clammy skin

Shallow, rapid breathing

Rapid heartbeat

If you experience any of these symptoms after an injury, here's what to do:

▶ **Call 911.** You need to get medical help quickly.

▶ **Lie down.** This will take as much physical stress off you as possible.

▶ **Stay warm.** Cover yourself with a blanket or coat to stay as comfortably warm as you can.

▶ **Raise your legs.** Prop them up about a foot off of the floor. This will help stabilize your circulation. At the same time, keep your head resting on the floor.

▶ **Remain calm.** Emotional stress can worsen the situation. Know that help is on its way and that you're going to be okay.

To treat first-degree and small second-degree burns that don't affect areas of the body listed above, take the following steps:

> **Take a pain reliever.** You can use aspirin, ibuprofen (Motrin, Advil), acetaminophen (Tylenol), or naproxen (Aleve).
> **Apply cold water.** Either hold the affected area under cold running water, which will help cool the burn, or apply cool, wet compresses. *Never use ice.* It can actually cause further damage to the skin.
> **Dress the wound.** Apply antibiotic ointment to the wound, and cover it with a nonstick bandage. This will keep the air off of it, reduce pain, and help prevent infection. Be careful to keep the bandage loose—you don't want it pushing or rubbing against the burn. If you have blisters, don't pop them. The best advice, unless your doctor tells you otherwise, is to leave them alone. The clear fluid in the blister may help the healing process. If the blister opens and drains on its own, cover it with antibiotic ointment and a nonstick bandage. The roof of the blister should not be removed, as it is protecting the wound.
> **Call your doctor.** If you have severe blistering, he or she may prescribe topical cortisone, which can help relieve pain and inflammation. If the pain is unbearable, if the wound is larger than three inches; or if your hands, feet, buttocks, groin, face, or major joints are affected, get to an emergency room. If you have suffered a burn from an electrical source, it's also a good idea to check in with a medical professional. Sometimes this type of burn will have little effect on the outer skin but can cause a lot of trouble internally.
> **Watch for infection.** Once the burn has begun to heal, keep an eye for signs of infection, such as green or yellow pus, further swelling, or a fever.

Serious burns require different treatment. If either you or someone nearby needs care for a third-degree burn, here is what to do:

> **Call 911.** It's important to get professional help on the scene as soon as possible.
> **Leave clothing in place.** Burnt clothing may be stuck to the skin, and trying to remove it can cause further injury.
> **Don't use cold water.** For third-degree burns, the sudden change in temperature can send the victim into shock.
> **Elevate the injury.** If possible, elevate the burned area above heart level to temporarily slow the blood flow to it.

Skin Facts: Did You Know?

As a burn heals, it can cause changes in the *pigmentation* (color) of your skin, and tanning can make those dark or light changes even more obvious! Keep burn wounds out of the sun as much as possible for at least a year, and apply sunblock or sunscreen to them when you can't avoid exposure.

> **Bandage with care.** Cover the burned area with a moistened sterile bandage, clean clothe, or clean towel, and gently lay it over the burned area until help arrives.

CHEMICAL BURNS

Combustion occurs when a fuel—such as the molecules in your skin—combines with oxygen in the air and produces heat, usually in the form of a flame. But combustion is not the only kind of burning we have to worry about. Some chemicals can also react with and do significant burn damage to your skin.

Although chemical burns happen most often on farms and in industrial settings where dangerous chemicals are more common, they happen often enough in the home to constitute a significant hazard that you should be aware of. Frequent causes of chemical burns in and around the house include:

> Ammonia
> Battery acid
> Bleach
> Cement mix
> Chemical fertilizers
> Denture cleansers
> Drain and toilet bowl cleaners
> Household cleansers
> Metal cleaners
> Pool chlorinators

Treating chemical burns is somewhat similar to treating combustion burns, but there are some important differences. Here is what to do:

Stop, Drop, and Roll

This is something we all learned as children, but it's good to remind ourselves of it once in awhile. If your clothes are on fire, the quickest way to put out the flames is to smother them. Fire can't burn without oxygen. So immediately drop to the ground and roll over like a log until the flames are completely out. If your hair is burning, you can use the same technique, or you can throw a heavy cloth over the flames and quickly pat them out. Do *not* use a light or flimsy cloth that can ignite easily.

- ▸ **Remove your garments.** Take off any clothing or jewelry that may still contain the chemical that caused the burn.
- ▸ **Clean the burn.** Run the wound under cold water for at least 20 minutes. This will help to flush away the toxin. However, if the chemical is in a powder form, such as lye or cement mix, brush as much of it off the skin as you can first. Some solid chemicals cause even more burning if they mix with water. If you know the offending chemical is an acid—for example, if it's a toilet-bowl or swimming-pool cleaner—you can use a mild soap as well as water to help remove it. If the chemical is an alkali, such as ammonia, you can first wash it with a vinegar solution before flushing it with water. Some industrial acids can not be easily removed with water, but you're unlikely to come into contact with them at home or school.
- ▸ **Apply compresses.** Lay a cool, clean, wet compress, cloth, or towel over the injury to relieve pain.
- ▸ **Bandage the wound.** Wrap the wound loosely in a sterile dressing.
- ▸ **Re-wash.** If the burning continues or starts again, hold the wound under running water for another 20 minutes. If it still doesn't stop hurting, or if the pain gets worse, get to an emergency room.
- ▸ **Call for help.** If your breathing becomes shallow, you feel shaky or faint, or you become very pale, call for help. You may be experiencing shock. Also, as with combustion injuries, second-degree chemical burns larger than three inches and all third-degree chemical burns require medical care, as do all burns occurring on the hands, feet, major joints, groin, buttocks, or face.

CALLUSES AND CORNS

Calluses and corns are actually the same thing: collections of dead skin that form a thickened pad in response to pressure and friction, usually on the palms of your hands or various surfaces on your feet. They often occur for the same reason blisters do: excessive rubbing. Treatment is simple. Foot calluses, whether they involve the toes, heel, or sole, can result from poorly fitting shoes, so make certain you ask for help to get a proper fit whenever you buy shoes. Also, be sure that new shoes feel comfortable. If your feet feel pinched or you notice rough surfaces rubbing against them, put the shoes you're trying back on the shelf. For your hands, wear gloves whenever you do anything that causes you to repeatedly grasp objects (sweeping, for example, or holding a softball bat).

To remove a callus or corn, soak it in warm water until it softens a bit, then pare it off with a coarse emery board or pumice stone. If the calluses are very thick, you can use salicylic acid pads, available at your local drugstore, to get rid of them.

FROSTBITE

If the air gets cold enough, it can freeze skin and underlying tissue. In other words, you develop frostbite. Frostbite can happen anywhere on the body, but most often it affects the fingers, toes, nose, chin, and earlobes. The symptoms include:

- ▶ Cold, numb skin that is hard to the touch
- ▶ Swelling of the affected area
- ▶ Color change (from normal to waxy pale to red to blue/purple)
- ▶ Blistering
- ▶ Slurred speech and confusion

If you develop frostbite, it is important to get to a hospital as soon as you can, even if the frozen skin thaws out. You will need treatment to prevent infection and limit tissue damage. If you don't get proper medical care, you could end up losing the affected body part—a finger, a toe, or even parts of your nose.

You can begin to warm the skin only if you're sure it won't refreeze, as thawing and then refreezing tissue will further damage it. You can start the thawing process by immersing the frozen body part in room-temperature water. Do *not* use hot or even very warm water, as the temperature will eventually cause intense pain. Refresh the water to keep it from growing too cold. If you can't get to a source of

Bloody Contact

If you have bloody contact with or exposure to someone else's open wound, talk to your pediatrician or doctor about it. They routinely test for bloodborne viruses such as hepatitis and HIV. But even if you are exposed to infected blood, there is no reason to panic. The risk of actually becoming infected is incredibly low from that kind of contact. Just be smart. See your doctor.

water, you can use body heat—holding your hands under your arm for frostbitten fingers, for example.

Do not rub frostbitten areas to thaw them. This will only cause more tissue damage. Also, don't hold frostbitten skin close to a fire or heating device. If you get too close to the heat source, your frozen nerve endings won't be able to feel the change in temperature, and you could end up with serious burn injuries.

PAPER CUTS

They can be so tiny that you can't see them, but paper cuts can give you a nasty, smarting pain that goes on for days. They hurt because they injure an area of skin, your fingertips, that are an extremely sensitive part of your body, containing a special type of nerve that is extraordinarily sensitive to light touch and pressure. Similar nerves appear in the lips, palms, nipples, and genitals.

But that's not the end of the story. A sheet of paper has a very sharp edge that can cut the skin—and, unfortunately, leave behind little bits of chemical-coated fibers made of wood mulch. These particles then irritate the pain-receptor nerves in the skin. To make matters worse, the cuts are usually so shallow that their edges begin healing very rapidly, trapping the fibers inside.

The best thing you can do for a paper cut is to flush it as thoroughly as you can with running water. It may also help to apply a little antibiotic ointment and cover it with a self-adhesive bandage.

To avoid paper cuts, square off the ends of piles of documents you're working with so that pages don't stick out. When working with envelopes, wear rubber finger protectors and use a letter opener.

RUNNER'S TOE

Runner's toe, tennis toe, and skier's toe are all names for the same condition: bleeding under a toenail that turns the nail black. It happens when a toenail keeps jamming against or catching on the inside of a shoe, and the nail slightly separates from the skin that holds it to the toe. It can be very painful, and the nail may eventually fall off.

Applying moleskin or padding over the injured toe can help relieve pain, but if the force of the blood pushing up against your toenail makes the discomfort unbearable, your doctor can drill a hole through it with a sterile needle to relieve the pressure. He or she may decide that removal of the nail is the best option.

If that happens, or if the nail falls off on its own, apply an antibiotic ointment to the injured area and wrap it comfortably with a bandage. Take ibuprofen or acetaminophen for pain. And don't worry: Unless your toenail's root has been removed, the nail will grow back.

Your best protection against runner's toe is to keep your toenails trimmed and wear shoes that fit properly. Shoes with a large toe box are best.

SPLINTERS

When one of these little slivers of wood, metal, thorn, or even bone penetrate and embed in the skin, it can feel like you've been poked with a hot razor blade. Usually, however, a splinter is more a nuisance than a real medical problem. If you have one that you can't easily pull out, the simplest treatment is no treatment at all. Over time, it will work its way free without any help. However, if it's uncomfortable and you want it gone, first try gently squeezing the skin on either side of it between two fingers. That may expose the end so you can grab it with a pair of tweezers.

If that doesn't work, you can "unroof" it. First, thoroughly wash your hands and the area over and around the splinter. Not only will that help prevent infection, but it will also soften up the skin to make the process easier. In fact, if the splinter is really buried, it may help to soak the affected area for 10 minutes before attempting to remove it. Next, sterilize a fine sewing needle and pair of tweezers by holding them in the tip of a flame for a few seconds and allowing them to completely cool. Scratch gently with the needle directly over the splinter until it lies exposed, and then remove it with the tweezers. Finally, apply some antibiotic ointment to the wound, and bandage it.

Do You Need Stitches?

To determine if you need stitches, consider the depth, width, and location of the wound.

> **Depth:** If the wound is deep and you see fatty tissue, you should see your doctor for evaluation and possible suturing.

> **Width:** If you can't easily hold the edges of the wound together and it gapes open, stitches may be needed for correct healing and to reduce the size of the scar.

> **Location:** If the wound is on your face and you are unsure if you need stitches, see your doctor, since stitches can give you a smaller or narrower scar. If the wound is over a joint or area that moves and stretches, stitches will help hold the skin together for better healing.

Stitches aren't the only option for closing a cut. Depending upon the wound's size and severity, your doctor may decide to use an alternative option, such as adhesive bandages called steri-strips, medical-grade superglue, or staples. Although stitches are sometimes used to help stop bleeding, profuse bleeding is not always a reason to get them. Some parts of our bodies, such as our scalps, lips, and mouth, bleed more than others, so a small wound can produce a lot of blood. In these areas, try applying pressure to the wound for 10 to 15 minutes before making a final decision to head for the ER. Finally, if you do need to have stitches, time is of the essence. You need to see a doctor within 24 hours. After that, it's too late to put them in.

Whether you remove the object or leave it alone, make sure to check every couple of days for signs of infection, such as surrounding redness, green or yellow drainage, extreme tenderness with red streaks extending away from the area, or a fever along with any of those symptoms.

Check with your doctor to make sure you're up-to-date with your tetanus boosters. You should have one every 10 years. If you're due or almost due, don't put it off: Now is the time to get one.

ALL ABOUT SCARS

Scars can be unsightly reminders of past injuries, surgeries, diseases, or acne. Fortunately, there are some things you can do to help the healing processes along, and with the right treatment, you can do a great deal to minimize the impact of a scar's appearance. Here are some steps you can take:

Use proper wound care. Cleaning and applying antibiotic ointment to cuts and abrasions will keep them moist, speed healing, and help prevent or minimize scarring.

Use sunscreen. If you do form a scar, using sunscreen can make it less noticeable. After the skin heals from a wound, some discoloration often remains afterward. The affected area of skin will look more pink, brown, or white, and that discoloration can last up to a year or longer before it fades. But eventually it *does* fade. Discoloration alone, however, is not a scar. A scar is permanent tissue change that goes deep into the skin's lower layer. Just like normal healing skin, however, it can become discolored. Keeping it coated with sunscreen after the initial healing phase is important, because UV ray exposure can actually make the discoloration last longer. So use an SPF 30 sunscreen on new scars whatever season it is, and be sure to reapply it regularly.

Massage your skin. You may also be able to limit scar tissue build-up by gently rubbing the area with the soft pads of your fingers for five-minute periods once or twice a day. Move your fingers in a circular motion over the scar, then push back and forth all along the scar's length. Finally, pinch one end of the scar gently between your thumb and first two fingers, then "walk" the pinch to the other end. Using a moisturizing cream as you massage can be helpful. This technique works best with new scars, but you should wait until a few weeks after initial healing has occurred and stitches have been removed before starting this.

Apply silicone. Some over-the-counter products that use silicone sheets to soften and flatten new scars may be effective. You can apply them after the initial wound is completely healed, and because they're flexible, you can use them on any part of the body. Generally, the treatment requires that you wear a silicone sheet over your scar for at least 12 hours a day for eight to 12 weeks.

Rest. For the first few months of healing after your injury or surgery, your doctor may want you to rest and stay away from some of your usual activities such as sports, dancing, or even gym class. This is really hard to do, but any trauma or extra stretching of a healing wound can make the scar bigger.

Scar removal. You can never completely remove a scar. But you can surgically alter it to make it less noticeable, and sometimes even replace it with a smaller scar. Here are some techniques currently available:

> - **Surgical alteration.** Cuts away older, wider scars and joins the skin back together in a less prominent way.
> - **Dermabrasion.** Uses a specialized machine to remove the top layer of skin. For deeper scars, several sessions may be necessary.
> - **Laser therapy.** Applies high-energy light beams to decrease the scar's redness or resurface the scar.
> - **Tissue fillers.** Uses injections of fat, collagen, or a man-made substances to level out indented scars such as those left by acne.
> - **Punch grafts.** Removes small scars and fills in the circular cut with small grafts of normal skin taken from elsewhere on the body.
> - **Chemical peels.** Uses chemicals to remove the top layer of skin. This approach is generally used only with superficial scars.

Keloids. A *hypertrophic scar* is one that is raised. A keloid is a scar that continues to form beyond the area of the initial wound. If you think you're developing a keloidal scar—that is, if a rapidly expanding, bumpy scar forms anywhere on your body—talk to your doctor about it. Catching a keloid early can help keep it under control.

Skin Facts: Did You Know?

The darker your skin, the greater your risk for forming keloid scars. Africans and people of African decent are most likely to get them, as are people of Asian descent. One study showed that among black individuals, 16 percent had developed at least one keloid.

The same kind of massage you would do for a hypertrophic scar can help reduce the impact of a keloid. So can applying silicone sheets. The most effective therapy, however, is to inject cortisone directly into the scar, which helps it flatten out. Some doctors will apply a *cortisone tape* instead of or in addition to injections. Surgical removal of a keloidal scar is rare, because the resultant scar often looks worse than the original.

If you tend to form keloids, don't pierce your ears or any other part of your body, and avoid getting a tattoo. The tendency toward keloid formation may be inherited, so if you have family members with keloids, you should consider yourself at risk for them and take the same precautions.

WHAT YOU NEED TO KNOW

- You can treat minor cuts and scrapes by stopping the bleeding, washing the wound, applying a topical antibiotic ointment, and applying a nonstick bandage.
- For major wounds—gaping cuts, abrasions that go below the skin or leave a large hanging flap—stop the bleeding with pressure, wash it off as best you can, apply an antibiotic ointment, and seek medical help.
- Burns fall into three categories. First-degree burns leave the skin red and swollen and may be painful. Second-degree burns create blisters, burn off the top layer of skin, and are very painful. Third-degree burns burn all the way through the skin. You can treat first-degree and minor second-degree burns with cold water and antibiotic ointment. Large second-degree burns and all third-degree burns require immediate medical attention. Many burns on the face, hands, feet, genitals, major joints, or buttocks require medical attention.
- For a chemical burn, flush away any remaining chemicals before treating the burn. If it is a dry powder, brush it away before flushing the burn site.
- Any bite that penetrates the skin should be evaluated by a doctor. Animals pose a risk of rabies as well as infection.
- Any close encounter with a bat—even if you don't see a bite mark—should be considered a bite and be evaluated immediately.
- Thawing of frostbitten skin should only be done with room-temperature water and only when you're sure the skin won't refreeze. Frostbite should *always* be evaluated and treated by a doctor, even if you've managed to successfully thaw the skin.

- Any wound that penetrates the skin can be an avenue for tetanus. Make certain that your boosters are on schedule.
- Splinters will usually work their way out on their own.
- You can minimize the appearance of scars through proper wound care, massage, and the use of scar-reducing products while the scar is still new.
- You can minimize keloidal scars with these techniques as well, but a doctor can help you with cortisone treatments.
- If you are prone to keloids or have family members who are, do not get piercings or tattoos.

5

Bites, Stings, and Rashes

Liz is at a party. The music is playing, the burgers are great, and the Sun is going down. A few kids are still swimming in the pool, but most are lying around, talking, laughing, flirting. Best of all, someone has just arrived who Liz really hoped would be there, someone who can put butterflies in her stomach just by smiling in her direction. Life is good. And then it happens. She starts to itch, and she can't stop swatting, shooing, and scratching. She looks around. No one else seems to be having the same problem. This is not the first time this has happened, so she knows it's only going to get worse unless she goes inside—where she'll probably end up alone. Why does this happen to her? And how can she make it stop?

BUG BITES

Severe itching can be one of the most excruciating and annoying sensations, short of extreme pain, that you will ever experience. But like pain, itching is there to protect you. In fact, the same nerves that transmit painful impulses to and from the brain also carry itch signals back and forth. Why, then, do you need these sensations?

Although pain and itching both designed to defend you from harm, they work in different ways. Pain motivates you to move away—quickly. If you touch a hot ember and burn your finger, your first instinct is to snatch your hand back. Itching, on the other hand, causes you to do the opposite: Instead of retreating, you move your hand toward the sensation, and then you scratch. That's because the culprit is often a toxin or insect either sticking to the surface of your skin or settled into its upper layer, and you instinctively try to scrape it away with your fingernails.

Does the strategy work? In fact, it does. Not only does scratching help clean the affected area, but it also sends a signal to your brain that you're working to get rid of the troublemaker. Your brain then rewards you by lessening the itch. And even if you can't entirely scratch away the problem, your fingernails may give you just enough pain to distract you from the itch. The downside to this response is that continued or vigorous scratching can tear the upper layer of skin and allow infection to occur. It may be difficult not to scratch if you have a fresh insect bite, but try your best to keep it to a minimum.

Among the most common causes of itching are insect bites. The little critters are drawn to you because you have some things they crave: warmth and blood. Although you may be your parents' favorite kid, a straight-A student, and generally a kind and considerate person, to a bedbug, mosquito, flea, or chigger, you're just today's dinner special.

Unfortunately, these bugs do more than simply relieve you of a drop of blood. They also leave you with some souvenirs. For one, when they penetrate the surface of your skin, some insects inject saliva that contains blood-thinning chemicals that keep their meal in liquid form. Very often, after repeated exposure to these pests, your body learns to warn you with a sudden sting or itch. Your first reaction, then, is to bring your hand to the area—where it either swats or shoos away the bug, then instinctively scratches the place that was just bitten.

As it turns out, that is a very smart thing to do, because the other memento that insects might leave behind with their saliva is serious disease. The quicker you can stop the attack and get rid of the toxin, the less exposure you have to potential infection.

Following is some information on the more common of these attackers, as well as some tips on treating their bites and keeping them out of your life.

BEDBUGS

They're gross, they're difficult to control, and they can leave you covered in maddeningly itchy bumps. Unfortunately, they're also becoming a fact of life for more and more people both in the United States and abroad.

Until just a few years ago, it seemed as if bedbugs had largely disappeared from America's bedrooms. That was because insecticides like *DDT* kept them at bay. Unfortunately for us, we have since learned that some of these chemicals harm the environment and pose a risk to human health, so they're no longer in use. Now that our use of chemical defenses is down, bedbugs have wasted no time in making an annoying comeback.

Today, they may show up not only where you sleep, but also in hotels, theaters, health clubs, hospitals, schools, and any other place that gives them access to their favorite prey—humans. They spread rapidly because they're small (about as long as a grain of rice); flat, so they can hide easily in crevices, cracks, and folds; and have a color—reddish brown—that gives them great camouflage. They can—and do—hitch rides in suitcases, trouser cuffs, and pet fur.

The good news is that these pests are more annoying than dangerous, as they're not known to infect humans with disease. In some people, however, they can cause an allergic blistering rash or giant hives, so they're not completely harmless.

If you're under attack from bedbugs, you probably won't realize it until after the fact, because along with blood-thinning saliva, they also inject a small dose of anesthetic into the skin, which numbs the area so you can't feel the bite. Your first clue will probably be the appearance of red, itchy bumps when you wake up from a nap or a long sleep.

Treatment. Simply apply a little cortisone 1% cream or ointment two or three times a day until the itching stops. If you have an allergic reaction with wheezing or throat swelling, get medical help immediately. Thankfully, a severe reaction like this to bedbugs is extremely rare. Also, do your best to refrain from scratching. Too much of it can set the stage for infection.

Prevention. As with many insect pests, prevention is your best strategy. Here are some ways to defend your home against these invaders:

> ▸ **Exterminate.** Ask your parents to call in an exterminator at the first hint of bedbugs.
> ▸ **Clean thoroughly.** Vacuum thoroughly at least once a week, especially around your bed. Don't leave piles of dirty clothes sitting out, and try not to create mounds of paper in your room—or anything else that could provide a hiding place.

➤ **Change linens.** You should put fresh sheets, blankets, and pillow cases on your bed every week. Wash the soiled ones in water that is 97°F or warmer.

➤ **Inspect.** If you go away on vacation or travel for any other reason, inspect all of your clothing and luggage *before* you bring it back into your home. The same goes for used articles of clothing, furniture, or anything else you acquire from outside of your home.

BEES, WASPS, AND ANTS

Many of us are afraid of snakes, but we take bees, wasps, and ants for granted. They're just part of the background, critters we see every day. But statistically, we have it all backward. Nearly four times more people die annually from bee stings than from snake bites in the United States. And in the deep South, fire ants cause the death of about 30 people every year.

All of these insects come from the same family, but of course, they have their differences. A honeybee, for example, can sting only once. Its stinger is barbed and anchors itself in the skin, so the bee can't pull it out. Instead, the bee leaves its stinger and venom gland behind and eventually dies. Wasps, bumble bees, and fire ants, on the other hand, have smooth stingers. They can—and do—sting over and over again. Yellow jackets and hornets, by the way, are types of wasps. In fact, they are the most aggressive types. All will attack to defend themselves or their nests.

Treatment. Bee and wasp stings produce immediate swelling, redness, and pain that can last up to two days. Fire ants produce a similar reaction, along with a white pustule at the sting site, but the inflammation will normally go away after about 45 minutes. The

Skin Facts: Did You Know?

A healthy adult who isn't allergic to bee stings can tolerate 10 stings for every pound of body weight.

problem with fire ants is that they are aggressive, and they tend to swarm, so multiple sting sites are common.

If you sustain a sting from any of these insects, move away from the hive or nest. Make certain you have no insects left on you, and get to a safe, sheltered area. If you have been stung by a honey bee, remove the stinger as quickly as possible, because the venom enters the skin for about 45 seconds after the sting. It probably doesn't matter how you get the stinger out, just get it out quickly and wash the area afterward. If you extract the stinger within 15 seconds, the sting will be less severe. For all stings, wash the wound and apply an ice pack to minimize swelling. Then swab on antibiotic ointment, and take oral diphenhydramine (Benadryl) if the itch is severe. Remember, Benadryl will make you drowsy, so don't ride a bike or drive a car after taking it.

The real danger in being stung by any of these insects is not so much in the power of the venom, but rather in *anaphylaxis,* a severe allergic reaction that can develop in some individuals—allergic shock that can be fatal. Symptoms of anaphylaxis include:

➤ Hives
➤ Wheezing, trouble breathing
➤ A feeling of throat swelling
➤ Swelling of the arms and/or legs
➤ Faintness
➤ Nausea
➤ Chest pain
➤ Slurred speech

Even if you have only one of these symptoms, it is important to get emergency medical attention immediately. Call 911. Lie down and try to remain calm while you wait. If the sting is on an extremity, you can tie a scarf or belt above it to slow the blood flow to your heart, but leave it loose enough to slide two fingers under it. Any sting that incurs in the throat or mouth needs immediate emergency medical attention.

People with a known allergy to bee stings should keep an emergency kit on hand. You will need a prescription to purchase one. These kits contain a medication called *epinephrine* (an EpiPen), which should be injected as quickly as possible after a sting occurs. The medication will help prevent anaphylaxis, but you still need to call 911.

Prevention. Obviously, it's best if at all possible to avoid stings in the first place. Here are some strategies that will help keep you out of harm's way:

Killer Bees

So-called "killer bees" are actually a hybrid of relatively gentle European honeybees and their far more aggressive cousins, African honeybees. Since a few of them escaped their hives and began reproducing in the wilds of Brazil in 1957, they have spread northward at a rate of 200 miles a year. Since that time, about 1,000 people have died as a result of killer bee attacks. The bees are now established in Southern and Western regions of the United States. Killer bees look like ordinary honeybees—brown with black stripes—but they're far more aggressive. They react to disturbances that other bees would ignore, and they attack in swarms in great numbers. Victims receive 10 times as many stings as a European bee would deliver, and killer bees will chase their victims over distances of a quarter mile. The best way to avoid attack is to stay away from all bees' hives and swarms, which should be reported to local authorities such as the police or pest control operators.

> **Walk carefully.** Wear shoes and be careful where you step. Yellow jackets can nest in the ground, and many bees hover low to find flower blossoms. If you live in Texas or the southeastern states, keep a special eye out for ant mounds. Disturbed fire ants will pour out by the hundreds and swarm whatever has bothered them. When they attack, they latch on with their mandible and sting over and over again. People who live in these areas have a 50 percent chance of sustaining an ant sting in any given year.

> **Don't wear perfume.** Sweet scents like perfume and cologne attract bees and ants.

> **Eat indoors.** Although it's fun to eat outside in nice weather, if bees or stinging ants are about, you're better off staying inside for your meal.

> **Seal your drinks.** Keep liquid refreshment tightly sealed with a lid when you're not drinking it. When you are drinking, do so from an open cup or glass so you can see what's going into your mouth. Insects have a nasty way of crawling into bottles and cans, where they're out of sight.

> **Cover waste.** Trash—especially food leftovers—should be discarded in a tightly sealed can, where insects can't get in and congregate.
> **Wear light colors.** Like mosquitoes, stinging insects have a harder time seeing lighter shades, but dark or bright colors attract them.
> **Don't swat.** If a bee is buzzing nearby, don't start swatting at it in the air. It may attack and even enlist a few of its buddies to help. If it won't leave you alone, move slowly and calmly indoors, where it can't follow.

CHIGGERS

Chiggers are tiny bugs that belong to the *arachnid* family—along with spiders, scorpions, and ticks. They are actually the *larva*e (baby bugs) of harvest mites, also called scrub mites. Although people believe they burrow into the skin and suck blood, they actually do neither. Instead, they attach to a hair follicle or skin pore, into which they release digestive chemicals. As a result, skin cells rupture and the chiggers feast on the fluids. All of this causes irritation to the surrounding skin, of course, and ends up leaving red, itchy bumps. That is likely to be the only symptom you see, as these larvae are too small to be seen by the naked eye. In the United States, chiggers are not known to carry disease, so while they may be gross, they're not dangerous.

Treatment. To treat chigger bites, clean the area with soap and water and apply cortisone 1 percent cream or ointment to reduce itching. Home remedies include painting the bite sites with fingernail polish, baby oil, and cold cream, but no one knows how effective they are since no one has done studies on them. However, it wouldn't hurt to try them.

Prevention. Chiggers like warm, moist places—such as the folds of your skin, especially under tight clothing. So one way to avoid them is to make yourself unappealing by wearing loose, cooling clothing. Showering immediately after a nature walk can also help wash chiggers away before they attach to you.

FLEAS

Unlike bedbugs, fleas don't consider humans their first choice for a meal. They prefer to feast on your dog or cat. But if your pet brings them into your house, you are now on their menu. Fleas will attack humans if they are the only source of blood available.

Flea bites usually appear as small, red, itchy bumps on the waist, ankles, and/or armpits, as well as the crooks of the elbows and backs of the knees. You may itch only where the bumps are, but in some people, the itchy sensation can extend beyond the bite site.

These insects do, on rare occasions, spread disease—primarily typhus, a bacterial disease that is easy to treat but can be lethal, especially to young children and the elderly, if not taken care of. Symptoms include headache, chills, fever, and rash. It is not directly contagious, but it can spread through a flea infestation in your home.

Treatment. As with bites from other blood-sucking *arthropods* (bugs), treatments consists of a little cortisone cream and cold compresses.

Prevention. The best way to cope with flea bites is to avoid them in the first place. Here is what to do:

- ▶ **Wear socks.** Your ankles are the easiest targets for fleas, so cover them up.
- ▶ **Launder your bedclothes.** Wash sheets, blankets, and pillow cases in hot water. Running them through several cycles may improve results. Do the same for your pet's bedding—or get rid of it and buy fresh items.
- ▶ **Shield your pets.** Repellants such as Frontline or Advantage for your dog or cat can keep them flea-free. You won't have these bugs in your house if they don't ride in on your pets.
- ▶ **Vacuum.** Vacuum carpets, rugs, and drapes, furniture, cushions, and bedding. Sweep everywhere else.
- ▶ **Exterminate.** Call in a professional exterminator to rid your home of these pests. Make sure young kids and pets are removed from the premises while the exterminator is spraying.

MOSQUITOES

Other than maybe a sudden thunderstorm, there is nothing that can ruin an evening patio party faster than a swarm of ravaging, blood-thirsty mosquitoes. If you're the type of person who smells tasty to them, you can quickly find yourself covered with red or whitish bumps that give a whole new meaning to the word "itch." And yes, from the mosquito's point of view, some people are tastier than others.

Skin Facts: Did You Know?

Only female mosquitoes bite people. They need a particular protein from blood that allows them to lay eggs. Male mosquitoes don't even have the mouth apparatus to penetrate the skin of an animal. They feed on flower nectar.

Over the 30 million years of their evolution, these critters have developed a keen set of tools to track down their prey. They carry around a sensing system that detects perspiration, heat, body odor, a chemical that builds up in your muscles called lactic acid, and carbon dioxide—which you give off with every breath you exhale. As it happens, certain people sweat more, have a stronger scent, and give off more carbon dioxide and lactic acid scent than others. You're more likely to belong to this select group of individuals if you're male, have type O blood, and/or are overweight.

When these insects bite, they use a long snout, called a *proboscis,* like a hypodermic needle to break the skin and draw blood out. If left to finish their meal, they will consume enough to double or triple the size of their abdomens before stopping.

Mosquitoes have been called the world's deadliest insect, and it's a well deserved reputation. Among its 2,700 species are some that carry *malaria,* yellow fever, *dengue fever,* and *encephalitis*—a brain inflammation also known as sleeping sickness. Each of these diseases has caused millions of deaths throughout human history.

Although in this country your chances of developing a serious disease from a mosquito bite is generally much lower than in some other parts of the world, one type of encephalitis, caused by the West Nile virus, has been gaining ground. In 2008, over 1,300 cases of West Nile were reported across the country, and 43 of them were fatal.

The mosquito usually picks the virus up from an infected bird, and then injects it into its next victim—often a human or horse. About one in five infected people actually show symptoms of any illness, but when they do, it can appear in two different forms. The first is the milder type, called West Nile fever (WNF). Its symptoms include moderately elevated temperature, head and body aches, enlarged lymph nodes, and a skin rash. WNF usually passes after a few days. The second type, full-blown West Nile virus encephalitis (WNVE), is much more severe, and individuals can experience headaches, high fever, stiff neck, confusion, weak muscles, convulsions, coma, and paralysis. The symptoms can last from weeks to months and can result in permanent brain damage—or, in worse-case scenarios, death.

Obviously, then, it's a good idea to protect yourself from mosquitoes as much as you can and to know enough to recognize the symptoms of WNF and WNVE.

Treatment. As with other itchy bug bites, you can treat these bumps with cortisone 1 percent cream or ointment and cool compresses. Calamine lotion may help as well, but stay away from topical products containing antihistamines. The skin will absorb them, and you will have no control over how much gets into your system. If the itching becomes unbearable, an over-the-counter antihistamine such as Benadryl may give you some relief. For use, follow the label instructions. Some people also suggest applying a baking soda paste. This may or may not work for you, but it wouldn't hurt to give it a try. Just mix enough baking soda with water to make a sticky paste and smear it on the bites. Reapply as necessary.

Symptom Checklist for Mosquito-Borne Diseases

Convulsions	Neck stiffness
Disorientation	Rash
Extreme tiredness	Sensitivity to light
Fever	Swollen lymph nodes
Headache	Vomiting
Muscle or joint aches	Yellow or orange skin or eyes
Nausea	

Prevention. There are some very effective ways to keep mosquitoes from making a meal of you, even if you're a person who usually attracts them. Here's how:

> ► **Armor yourself.** If you can, wear long-sleeved shirts and trousers instead of tee shirts and shorts. The less skin you expose, the better. Also, wear light colors. Believe or not, mosquitoes have a harder time seeing them.
> ► **Apply repellant.** Americans have been using *DEET* (NN-diethyl-meta-toluamide) to repel mosquitoes for over 50 years. In fact, the U.S. Department of Health and Human Services' Centers for Disease Control and Prevention recommends its use. Despite rumors that it causes brain damage and cancer and has other unwelcome side effects, researchers have demonstrated again and again that that it is very safe and extremely effective for people over the age of two months. DEET works by confusing the mosquito's sensory system, which makes you, for all practical purposes, invisible to it. In other words, the little vampires just can't find you! If you're one of the rare individuals with a sensitivity to DEET, you can try products containing oil of lemon eucalyptus or a chemical called *picaridin*. However, unlike DEET, apply picaridin to clothes only, *never* on skin. It is toxic to the human nervous system.
> ► **Remove habitats.** Basically, you need to get rid of any nearby standing water, because that's where mosquitoes make their homes. Check gutters, flowerpots, old tires, and any other place water collects. Change the water in children's pools and birdbaths every week.

Many people swear by citronella candles, electric bug zappers, and so-called "bug lights," but no one knows how effective they really are.

SCORPIONS

Scorpions look menacing, and Hollywood certainly takes every opportunity to portray this bug as a deadly, eight-legged monster, but the fact is that in the United States, the species is unfairly maligned. Only one American variety, the straw-colored bark scorpion *(Centruroides exilicauda or sculpturatus)*, which lives in Arizona, New Mexico, and parts of California, has a dangerously toxic sting. Even that species causes very few deaths among teens and adults—but stings in children under age five are very dangerous and potentially lethal. That's not to say all of the other 29 species who live here are cuddly, exactly, but their stings are likely to result in little more than some

Applying DEET

Using DEET is a safe and effective way to avoid the bites of bloodsucking insects, including mosquitoes, ticks, gnats, mites, and horse flies. Still, it's an active chemical, and misuse can lead to poisoning, so abiding by the following rules of proper application is important:

- ▸ **Choose the appropriate product.** DEET formulations come in many strengths. Those that work best for teens (and adults) fall in the 15 to 40 percent range. Younger children should use 8 to 10 percent products.

- ▸ **Dress for protection.** Cover as much of your skin as possible with clothing. The less exposure you have to DEET or any chemically active substance, the better.

- ▸ **Apply sparingly.** These products also come in different forms: liquid, lotion, and spray. Pour liquids and lotions onto your palm first, and spread it evenly with your hand over *exposed areas only*. Do not apply it to skin that is covered by clothing. When using the spray, hold it six to eight inches from your skin, and again, apply only to exposed areas. *Never* apply the spray directly to your face. Spray a little on your palm and spread it over your cheeks, forehead, ears, and neck. Don't get it into your eyes, nose, or mouth. If you're putting DEET on your baby brother or sister, don't apply it to their hands: Children put their hands in their mouths, and the chemical can be toxic when swallowed.

- ▸ **Don't overdo.** You don't need to saturate your skin with DEET. Use only enough to form a minimal layer of protection. You can reapply it if you have been swimming.

- ▸ **Remove it.** Wash your hands after applying it, and be sure to shower and remove all of it once you're indoors and no longer exposed to biting bugs.

- ▸ **Avoid clothing and plastic.** DEET can damage plastic-based products, including Spandex and rayon. Avoid getting it on the frames of your glasses. It can also harm leather, furniture finishes, watch crystals, paint, and varnish. It won't hurt nylon or wool.

pain, minor swelling, and tenderness at the wound site. The bark scorpion's sting, on the other hand, can cause intense pain; profuse salivation; excitability; unusual eye, head, and neck movements; and numbness or tingling around the sting.

Treatment. For most scorpion stings, a cold compress followed by antibiotic ointment is usually all you need. For bark scorpion stings, you may need an intravenous sedative, so you should go to a clinic or emergency medicine facility. In Arizona, you can get an *antivenin*—a medication that neutralizes the poison in the sting—but some people have reported an allergic reaction to it. For any scorpion sting that occurs outside of the United States, get emergency medical help immediately. Many very deadly species do exist in the world, including some in Mexico.

Prevention. These critters don't want to sting you. In fact, they would much rather avoid people and attack only when threatened—such as when a human foot descends from above. If you live in an area where scorpions are common, always check your shoes, clothing, and bedsheets before you get into them. Check backpacks and open purses as well. Keep windows and doors closed tightly, if possible, and avoid walking barefoot. Use a flashlight when you're out at night. Part of the bark scorpion's plating is florescent and will glow in the light.

SPIDERS

Spiders get a bad rap. Whenever someone wakes up with unexplained bumps and red marks on an arm or leg, "spider bite" is often the first conclusion jumped to. Some people even believe that if your mouth hangs open during a deep, sound sleep, you're sending an invitation to nearby arachnids to crawl in and enjoy the warmth. Why do we create these fictions?

Well, spiders *do* look a little alien; we know that they're top predators in their little worlds; and in fact, some are dangerous. But most of the species you will run into during your day-to-day life are benign—and even beneficial, as they help control insect populations. In any case, it has been said that no matter where you are—excluding the polar ice caps—you're always within three feet of a spider, so it's best to accept them and learn to coexist with them. And the next time you wake up with little red bumps, think bedbugs.

In the United States, we have two dangerous species: the black widow and the brown recluse.

Black widow. The females of this species carry an extremely potent *neurotoxin,* a venom that affects your central nervous system, but they inject so little that teens and adults rarely die from it. Males and baby black widow spiders are harmless.

In the southern and western United States, these spiders tend to live in garages, tool sheds, and crawl spaces—dark places where they can remain undisturbed. They also weave their webs in logs and piles of stone or rubble. Northern varieties rarely live indoors. They prefer to live away from people, in areas of scrub and sparse vegetation.

The female of the species has a round, shiny black abdomen, with a telltale hourglass mark on the underside. The hourglass may be yellow, orange, or red. Females can measure an inch and a half in length with their legs extended. Some varieties have red spots on the backs of their abdomens as well. Males are about half that size and sport white lines that radiate outward on the underside of the abdomen.

Reaction to a black widow bite varies from person to person. At first, some people feel immediate, horrendous pain. Others feel almost nothing but a little pinprick sensation. Eventually, however, as the poison spreads, the discomfort can become pretty acute, especially in the abdomen and back, and breathing may become difficult. Victims can also become nauseated, sweat profusely, develop tremors, experience an increase in blood pressure, and develop a fever. Generally, symptoms will go away after a day or so, even if left untreated, but small children, older people, and individuals with weak hearts or other health problems can be at risk for more serious outcomes or even death. Generally, the only first aid you can perform is to place cold compresses on the bite site, which usually consists of two tiny red fang marks, to help reduce swelling. Otherwise, get emergency

Skin Facts: Did You Know?

Although the black widow is named for the female's supposed habit of eating its partner after mating, that rarely happens. Generally, the male will exit the web immediately after fertilization, before the female's instincts switch back from reproductive to predator mode—when she'll eat anything smaller than she is.

care. A doctor may be able to give you medication that will reduce the pain. Bring the spider, alive or dead, in a jar if you can.

Tips for prevention include using common sense. If you live in an area where black widows are common, shake out your shoes and clothing before getting dressed. Wear gloves when handling any objects that might make an attractive nesting place for spiders—logs, rocks, boxes, etc. Your parents can seal your home by caulking cracks and installing door and window screens. Rid the house and environs of old piles of any kind of debris, natural or man-made, and remove old containers and cartons.

Brown recluse. These spiders live in the midwestern and southern United States, and they tend to make their nests in people's houses and immediate environs. That's because they're attracted to the large number of prey insects that crawl and fly around light bulbs. The brown recluse likes to hide (hence its name) in cracks, crevices, flower pots, tree boles, or any other cranny it can find.

The recluse is a long-legged spider with a distinctive violin-shaped mark on its back. The neck of the violin points toward the bulb of the spider's abdomen. With its legs extended, the recluse is about the size of a quarter. Both males and females are poisonous.

This spider's bite does most of its damage at the site where it occurs. However, not everyone bitten actually suffers harm. Some people have no reaction to the venom at all. They don't even feel the bite. Others not only feel it, but experience immediate, severe pain. Rarely, a victim will also develop restlessness, itching, fever, nausea, vomiting, or shock. Often, a small blister forms at the bite site, and the area around it gradually swells and turns red. The entire lesion, including the blister, then feels hard to the touch. The typical bite will grow to nearly three inches in length and half that in width. In some individuals, the bite will ulcerate and destroy surrounding skin. Gangrene can become a problem. In rare cases, it may take months for the wound to heal, and the victim can be left with significant scarring. The only treatment is to apply cold compresses to the bite to reduce swelling. If you suspect you have been bitten, save the spider, alive or dead, in a jar and bring it with you to the emergency room. Proper identification of the spider will help with treatment.

Avoiding the bites of these spiders is very important, as there is no antivenin for the brown recluse, and treatment is only marginally effective. In your house, caulk cracks and gaps around windows and in walls. Install screens and door sweeps. Get rid of debris piles and old containers both in and around your home.

TICKS

Ticks are arachnids, eight-legged creatures with no antennae, which makes them more closely related to spiders and scorpions than to six-legged insects like bedbugs and *lice.* Although the bite of this bug is usually painless and may not cause you to itch, it puts the victim at high risk for many diseases.

Ticks range in size from the nearly microscopic to about one-eighth of an inch long, but the larger varieties can engorge themselves with so much blood that they can bloat up to a half-inch in length. All ticks fall into two broad categories: hard and soft. A hard tick has armor plating on its back that makes it almost impossible to kill by simply stepping on it. This variety includes dog ticks, deer ticks (the ones that transmit Lyme disease), wood ticks, and Lone Star ticks. Soft ticks are rounder, and don't have protective back plating. Their

Tickborne Diseases

Ticks carry many different illnesses, many of which are quite serious. Here are the most common:

▶ **Babesiosis.** A sometimes deadly infection caused by a microscopic parasite that damages red blood cells.

▶ **Ehrlichiosis.** A bacteria that attacks white blood cells and produces an illness similar to, but not as serious as, *Lyme disease.*

▶ **Lyme disease.** A bacterial disease that can cause fever, rash, swollen joints, heart damage, and brain damage.

▶ **Rocky Mountain spotted fever.** A serious bacterial disease that causes fever, nausea, vomiting, headache, rash, abdominal pain and joint pain. It can also cause some long-term or permanent health problems.

▶ **Tularemia.** A highly infectious bacterial disease of humans, rodents, and rabbits that, depending upon the type, ulcerates the skin and can damage the lungs, digestive tract, throat, tonsils, lymph nodes, and eyes.

bites can be very painful, and they transmit disease quickly—within an hour of contact.

Generally, people pick up ticks by brushing against an infested plant, especially in wooded areas. When ticks bite, they attach firmly and can take days to finish their meal. That long exposure is one reason they're so good at transmitting disease.

Treatment. If a tick attaches to you, you will need to remove it. *Do not* use a hot match head, nail polish, gasoline, paint, or petroleum jelly for this purpose, as you might make the situation worse by damaging your skin. Instead, sterilize a pair of tweezers with a flame or alcohol, and then use them to flip the tick over on its back and grab it as close to your skin as possible. Pull gently until the tick comes free. Don't tug sharply or twist, as either of these actions might separate the body from the head and mouth parts, leaving part of the parasite in your skin and increasing your risk of infection. When the bug is completely removed, there should be a tiny, empty hole at the bite site. If anything is left in it, see a doctor to get help with complete removal. Wash the wound thoroughly with soap and water, and apply a topical antibiotic. Keep an eye out over the next few days for the appearance of any rash or other sign of infection. In disposing of the tick, don't touch it with your fingers or try to destroy it. Instead, simply flush it down the toilet. You can also trap it in a tightly sealed jar so that if you later show any signs of illness, a doctor can examine the tick.

Prevention. To avoid tick bites, cover as much of your exposed skin as you can before walking in areas that are wooded or contain tall grass or weeds. Then apply DEET (see box on page 87), which has proven effective for this use. When walking along a path, try to stay in the center so that you don't brush against the foliage on either side. Finally, inspect your clothing and skin every couple of hours. Do the same favor for your pets. If you find a tick that has not yet attached itself, remove it with tweezers or sticky tape. Don't touch it with your bare hands, as their secretions can contain disease.

CONTACT RASHES

You can't blame bugs for every itch and rash that happens to you, of course. Sometimes just brushing up against the wrong object can cause irritation and inflammation. These so called "contact rashes" are actually allergic reactions, known to doctors as *allergic contact dermatitis*. They happen when cells in your skin react to irritating

Lyme Disease

Probably the best known of all tickborne diseases is Lyme disease, named after the town of Lyme, Connecticut, where it was first identified in a group of children who had all mysteriously developed symptoms of arthritis. Lyme disease can be a serious illness, transmitted by black-legged ticks, that can affect the joints, heart, and brain. With early treatment, however, it can usually be controlled and cured. If you believe you have Lyme disease, it is important to see a physician as soon as possible. Here is what to look for:

> - **Bull's-eye rash.** From three to 30 days after a tick bite, a circular rash may develop around the wound and gradually expand to a diameter of 12 inches or more. Sometimes, the center of the rash fades, making it look like a bull's-eye. The medical name for this rash is *erythema migrans*.

> - **Flu-like symptoms.** Some people experience fatigue, chills, fever, headache, muscle pain, joint aches, and enlarged lymph nodes, either with or without the bull's-eye rash.

> - **Severe aches, pains, and other unusual symptoms.** After a few weeks, an untreated person may experience slackness on one or both sides of the face (Bell's palsy), severe headaches and/or stiff neck, changes in heartbeat, dizziness, and pain that travels from joint to joint.

> - **Joint pain.** A few months after the infection begins, severe joint pain and swelling may appear.

> - **Neurological symptoms.** Months, or sometimes years, after harboring untreated Lyme disease, you can develop numbness, shooting pains, tingling in the hands and feet, memory problems, and difficulty concentrating.

Early Lyme disease is easy to treat with antibiotics, but some people experience symptoms such as fatigue and joint pain for years after the infection is gone. This may be due to an autoimmune reaction—where the body's immune system attacks healthy tissue by mistake—triggered by the disease.

substances, called antigens, by releasing a chemical called *histamine* into the skin. The histamine activates nerves that then send itch signals to the brain. The two most common of these rashes are a reaction to metal, nickel dermatitis, and a reaction to plants in the poison ivy family, *Rhus dermatitis.*

Nickel dermatitis. Nickel is a metal used in just about everything, including earrings, necklaces, body piercing jewelry, buckles, snaps, coins, watchbands, eye frames, cell phones, and many other everyday items that touch your skin. You have probably been rubbing up against it for most of your life. An allergy to nickel, however, can suddenly develop at any age, and once you have it, you have it forever. With some allergens, repeated exposure weakens the allergic effect. Not so with nickel. In fact, the more you touch the metal, the worse your allergy will become.

The rash may be red, dry and scaly, bumpy, or blistering, and the itch can become severe. Generally, the inflammation will appear only where you have had contact with the metal, but in rare cases, it may appear on other areas of your body as well. Most often it will appear as an itchy rash around your belly button where your zipper, snaps, and belt buckles rub, but it can also show up on your earlobes, neck, or any other place where a metal object comes into contact with your skin.

You can care for mild cases of nickel dermatitis with over-the-counter hydrocortisone 1 percent cream, cool compresses, and Benadryl. For more serious or stubborn cases, you may want to see a physician, who can treat you with a prescription mid-potency topical steroid and Benadryl.

Preventing a contact allergy is a matter of avoiding the allergen, but that isn't always such a simple task. For nickel, start with your clothing. Cover all snaps with clear nail polish, then duct tape. Use scarves for belts, or wear only belts with plastic or leather covering the buckles. Turn clothing inside out to check for metal fasteners. You won't always know when jewelry or a new cell phone contains nickel, but you can find out with an inexpensive spot-testing kit available at pharmacies and from the Web. These kits contain two chemicals, dimethylglyoxime and ammonium hydroxide, that are applied to metal objects with a swab. If nickel is present, the swab will turn pink.

Rhus dermatitis (poison ivy, poison sumac, poison oak). Rhus dermatitis is named for a genus of plants that includes poison ivy, poison oak, and poison sumac. All of these secrete a substance called urushiol that produces a maddening itch and blistering rash

What Are Hives?

Hives are those spongy bumps, often ringed in red, that pop up when you're allergic to something. Doctors sometimes call them urticaria and consider them acute (short-term) if you've had them for fewer than six weeks, or chronic (long-term) if you've had them for longer than that. They can occur from exposure to sudden cold, exposure to sunlight, viral infections, medications, and from unknown causes. Hives can be as small as a pea or so large (giant hives) that they cover an entire arm or leg. They occur when a release of histamines—an immune-system response—causes tiny blood vessels in the skin, called capillaries, to leak fluid into surrounding tissue. The fluid then irritates nearby nerves, causing an itch. The hives disappear when the fluid is reabsorbed. They itch because the fluid irritates nerves in the epidermis. When the fluid leaks into deeper layers of tissue (the dermis), a condition called angio-edema occurs. If this happens on your face or neck, it can make your lips and throat swell. In worst-case scenarios, angioedema can be life threatening. Treatment of urticaria most often includes antihistamines such as Benadryl. For severe cases, where angioedema or anaphylaxis (swelling, wheezing, and trouble breathing) occurs, epinephrine, a natural hormone that helps the body cope with stress, and oral steroids are used.

that can last for weeks. Poison ivy and poison sumac grow mostly east of the Rocky Mountains in the form of vines or shrubs. Poison ivy grows as a plant, weed, or thick woody vine with three-leaf clusters, which may or may not be ridged along the edges. It may also produce green or white berries. Poison sumac typically grows as a bush or small tree in boggy and swampy areas in the South. It has seven to 10 rounded leaves growing in a row on either side of an upward-pointing stem. Poison oak commonly grows as a low plant or bush with three leaf clusters, but the leaves look somewhat like oak tree leaves. All of these plants may have an oily, glossy appearance.

Although it may take a few weeks, this rash will go away on its own. You can, however, help to keep symptoms under control by taking a few simple steps:

> **Wash off the plant oil.** For best results, do this right after exposure. Use soap and warm water. You might also want to change clothes, in case they have some of the oil on them.
> **Apply compresses.** Cold and wet are best. Apply several times a day for about a half hour for the first three days.
> **Use a steroid cream.** Try over-the-counter strength first. If it doesn't work, see your doctor about getting some prescription-strength medication. He or she may decide that oral medications are more appropriate.
> **Soak in oatmeal.** Short Aveeno baths can sometimes help. (Aveeno contains *colloidal oatmeal,* which soothes the skin.)
> **Take Benadryl.** Antihistamines can help relieve the itch and help you sleep. Do not drive or ride your bike if you take this.
> **See a doctor.** If the rash is widespread, is in or near your eyes, or produces an amber-colored crust, see a physician.

Note: Although many sources suggest using calamine lotion, it really dries out your skin, which can make you feel even worse. If you try it, use it sparingly and only for the first three days.

Preventing Rhus dermatitis is largely a matter of avoiding the offending plants. Despite what you may have heard, the rash is *not* contagious. However, if you still have some of the urushiol resin on your skin and it rubs onto someone else, they may develop the full-blown rash. Here are some other tips:

> **Stay on the beaten path.** It's not always easy to see what plants you're brushing against in the woods, so stay on cleared trails if you can.
> **Keep your pets in cleared areas.** Dogs and cats can rub against these plants, then transfer the irritating oils to you.

Skin Facts: Did You Know?

Ten percent of lost work time at the U.S. Department of Agriculture and Forestry Services is due to poison ivy, oak, or sumac rashes. Among the general population, these three plants cause more contact dermatitis than all other allergens combined.

The Mango–Poison Ivy Connection

The tropical mango is a favorite among many Americans, but if you're allergic to poison ivy, you might want to think twice about handling the mango's skin. It contains a substance very much like urushiol, which causes the poison ivy skin rash. Because the chemical is so similar to the irritating oil of the poison ivy plant, the body develops a "cross-reaction" to it—that is, it reacts as if it were the same oil. To avoid problems, let someone else remove the skin for you before enjoying the pulp of this fruit.

> **Clear plants from areas of high use.** In other words, get these things out of your yard. You might want to suggest that your parents call in professionals to do it.
> **Do not burn.** Never, ever burn poison ivy, oak, or sumac, even if the plants have been removed from the soil and are dead. The smoke from the fire will carry the resin, which can find its way into your eyes, mouth, and throat.
> **Wear gloves.** When handling this stuff, wear rubber gloves. Do not, however, wear latex. Urushiol can penetrate it.
> **Wear a barrier cream.** This should be a "must do" whenever you go walking in the woods. Your local drugstore will carry brands, such as Ivy Block, that will keep your skin protected. Wash off and reapply it every four hours for maximum effect.

JELLYFISH

Jellyfish are a hazard wherever sand meets water. In the Chesapeake Bay area alone, over half a million people are stung each year. The sting comes from venomous sacs, called *nematocysts,* located all along the floating tentacles these animals use to catch prey. While some species, such as Australia's box jellyfish (sea wasp), are deadly, the common varieties found in the United States are more likely to produce temporary discomfort in the form of tenderness, intense stinging or burning, and itching, with welts or a rash along the area of contact. Some people will progress to a more general reaction that

The Portuguese Man-of-War

This creature, also called a *bluebottle,* is actually not a jellyfish. It's a combination of four different organisms working together. Like a jellyfish, however, it uses tentacles to capture prey. In the United States, it occurs mostly in Hawaii and along the coasts of Florida and Texas, but it can show up anywhere—sometimes in schools of thousands! The man-of-war's sting is extremely potent and painful and has been known to kill people—although rarely a healthy teen or adult. Deaths occur more often among children and the elderly. In the water, the man-of-war looks somewhat like a balloon made of blue, pink, or violet gelatin with a fin on top. It will also trail long, threadlike blue tentacles beneath the water's surface. The only immediate treatment for a sting is to remove tentacles from the skin with tweezers or any other tool (but not your bare fingers), and continuously rinse the wound with freshwater until it disappears—the opposite of regular jellyfish sting treatment. Do *not* use vinegar, ammonia, or alcohol. If you have trouble breathing or show any other signs of illness, get emergency medical care right away.

can include nausea, diarrhea, vomiting, swollen lymph nodes, and abdominal pain. Rarely, a victim can experience difficulty breathing, fall into a coma, or have a fatal outcome.

Jellyfish are not aggressive animals. They simply spread their tentacles and float. Contact with humans is completely accidental.

Treatment. A jellyfish stings hurts immediately and will leave a slimy, burning substance on your skin. Your best bet is to grab a handful of sand and rub it over the sting until all of the slime is gone. Use vinegar, vodka, rubbing alcohol, or diluted ammonia (four parts water to one part ammonia) to rinse the wound. Meat tenderizer and even wet beach sand will also work. Do *not* wash the sting with freshwater, do not rub the area, and do not apply cold compresses, as any of these can activate nematocysts left in your skin and make the stinging worse. Next, use tweezers or gloves—not your bare fingers—to pull out any broken tentacles left above the skin. Then, to remove bits of tentacles from under the skin, apply shaving cream or a baking soda paste to the area and shave it with a safety razor. Finally, rinse again with any one of the liquids mentioned above, leaving it on for 15 to 20 minutes before patting the area dry.

Seek medical care if any symptoms occur beyond stinging, localized rash, and pain, or if the sting occurred in the mouth, throat, eye, or genitals.

Prevention. The best prevention for jellyfish stings, of course, is to stay out of the water when large numbers of jellyfish have been reported and avoid dead jellyfish that wash up on the beach—they don't have to be alive to hurt you. Walk on the dune side of any jellyfish you see in the sand. That will help you avoid stepping on its tentacles, which will most likely trail toward the water. If you're scuba diving, wear a wet suit and gloves. Jellyfish tend to congregate in larger numbers toward evening, so keep an eye out for them toward the end of the day.

SAND FLEAS

These little creatures are actually crustaceans, like crabs, lobsters, and shrimp, but they're very tiny, and when they attack humans, they feed like mosquitoes—they suck blood from your ankles and legs and leave a little saliva behind that causes itching and stinging with welts or hives.

Treatment. As with a bug bite that itches, wash the area, then apply cool, wet compresses and some hydrocortisone 1 percent cream or ointment.

Prevention. Avoid walking along beaches and other sandy areas in the evening or very early morning, as this is when sand fleas tend to be most active. When they gather together, they make a characteristic

Skin Facts: Did You Know?

The Arctic jellyfish is the largest in the world. Its tentacles can extend 200 feet—two-thirds the length of a football field.

Pityriasis Rosea: The Mystery Rash

Have you ever experienced a large, pink, scaly patch that suddenly appeared on your chest or back, followed by more of the same on your trunk and extremities a week or two later? If so, you may have had pityriasis rosea, a rash with no known cause—at least not among the bacteria, fungi (although it can look like ringworm), allergies, or internal diseases we know of. Some researchers believe it may be due to a virus, but as yet there is no hard evidence. Although about half the people who develop this condition do experience some itching, over-the-counter skin lotions or cortisone cream is usually enough to bring it under control. Fortunately, pityriasis rosea always goes away on its own, without permanent scarring, after six to eight weeks. The rash is not contagious and usually occurs only once in a lifetime.

high-pitched whining noise. If you hear anything like that, give it a wide berth.

SEABATHER'S ERUPTION

This is an extremely itchy, papular (pimply) rash that erupts from the skin after you have been in seawater for an extended period. It usually occurs under bathing suits. Scientists believe the condition is a reaction to the larvae (babies) of the thimble jellyfish. The swimsuit presses the tiny creatures against your skin, and they release venom in response. The most common symptom is intense itching that lasts for about a week. Some people also experience fatigue and a fever. Small children sometimes also experience diarrhea, nausea, or abdominal pain.

Treatment. Usually, over-the-counter corticosteroid or prescription cream and a little oral Benadryl is all you need for this condition, although some people say that rinsing with vinegar or alcohol also helps.

Prevention. The only way we know of to help prevent seabather's eruption is to shower with your swimsuit off as soon as you come out of the water for the day.

SWIMMER'S ITCH

Swimmer's itch is a reaction to a parasite that lives in permanent bodies of water—either fresh or marine. The parasite spreads through snails that releases it during a critical phase of its life cycle. Although it can penetrate human skin, it does not reproduce there or cause serious infection, and it is not contagious from one person to another. The only symptom is an itchy rash.

Treatment. There is no standard of care for swimmer's itch, and none is really necessary, but treating the itch with cool compresses and over-the-counter or prescription hydrocortisone cream and oral Benadryl might make it more tolerable. The rash usually reaches maximum size within the first 24 hours, and the itch will generally disappear within a week.

Prevention. Preventing this infection is simple: Dry off briskly with a towel over your entire body after swimming, rather than allowing the moisture to evaporate off of your skin. The wiping motion will whisk away parasites. Swimming farther from shore, if it's safe to do so, can also be helpful, as the parasites tend to live close to land. Since snails spread the parasites, don't swim in water where many snails accumulate. And since the parasites also affect many species of birds, don't encourage feathered friends to congregate where you swim by feeding them.

Heat Rash

Also known as prickly heat or miliaria rubra, heat rash can appear after a brief exposure to hot weather, but it's more likely to show up on an individual who has been living in torrid conditions for several months. The red rash is bumpy and can become very itchy. It occurs when a sweat gland becomes blocked and perspiration remains trapped under the skin, where it causes irritation. Most often, just spending time in cooler temperatures will relieve the rash. No other treatment is usually necessary. Because these blockages reduce sweating, heat exhaustion and heat stroke can be a problem, although rarely.

WHAT YOU NEED TO KNOW

➤ Always check your belongings after traveling before bringing them into your home. You want to make certain no unwelcome critters move in with you.

➤ Many itchy bug bites, such as those inflicted by mosquitoes and bedbugs, can be treated with soap and water, followed by cool compresses and over-the-counter hydrocortisone cream.

➤ Any signs of fever or other general symptoms of illness, such as aches, pains, fever, or unusual rashes after sustaining mosquito bites or a tick bite should be discussed with your doctor.

➤ Always use tweezers to remove a tick, and pull it directly and gently out without twisting. If any parts are left in the skin, have a doctor help you remove them. Never use your fingers.

➤ Proper use of DEET can deter mosquitoes, ticks, and other blood-sucking bugs from attacking you.

➤ Scorpion stings and spider bites are serious but usually not fatal. Still, changes in mental state, nausea, or other unusual symptoms should be evaluated immediately by a physician.

➤ The best protection against poison ivy, poison oak, and poison sumac is a barrier cream formulated specifically for that purpose and available at your local pharmacy.

➤ The rash caused by poison ivy, poison oak, and poison sumac is not contagious.

➤ Treat jellyfish stings with alcohol or vinegar but never with freshwater. Treat Portuguese man-of-war stings with freshwater but never alcohol or vinegar. Never pull the tentacles of either out with your fingers.

➤ Giant hives, swelling in the throat or mouth, or difficulty breathing after a bite, sting, or unusual rash is a medical emergency. Call 911.

6

Chronic Conditions: Skin Problems That Don't Go Away

Kim looked nervous, as if she were expecting very bad news. She sat upright on the doctor's examining room table with her arms crossed in front of her and her hands tucked away so they couldn't be seen. Her stare was fixed on the floor, and her mouth turned down in a pout. Her mom, sitting next to the table, tapped her foot impatiently. The doctor gently reached out and extended Kim's right arm to examine it.

"I don't know what you're so worried about," Kim's mother said. "People get these rashes all the time, and you used to have this when you were a baby. I'm sure Dr. Brown has some cream that will make it disappear as if it had never been there."

Dr. Brown didn't reply. She carefully touched the scaly, red patch in the crook of Kim's elbow and examined a similar spot on the back of her hand. "Does it itch a lot?" she asked.

Kim only nodded. Her eyes grew a little teary. "I can't sleep, and it looks terrible."

"It's really hard, I know," Dr. Brown said.

Kim shrugged and forced an expression of indifference.

"There's nothing to worry about," Dr. Brown said. "You're going to be okay."

"You see?" Kim's mother said. "I told you. The doctor will clear it right up."

Dr. Brown looked from daughter to mom. "Yes, we can find the right medicine that works for you to clear up the rash and control it," she said, "but I have to be honest with you. This is eczema. While

103

we do have great treatments, we don't have a cure that keeps it from coming back"

Kim's mother frowned. "I'm not sure I like what I'm hearing," she said. "Are you sure about this? When she was younger, her pediatrician told me that kids outgrow this."

"What your doctor said is true," Dr. Brown said, "but sometimes it gets better and then comes back later in life," She turned to Kim. "Are you okay?"

Kim now looked more thoughtful than upset. "Will this ever go away, or is this for the rest of my life?"

"A lot of people seem to outgrow it, but I can't make you any promises."

"Maybe we should get a second opinion," Kim's mother put in.

"That never hurts," Dr. Brown said.

Nearly every young person has a skin condition at some point in his or her life, whether it is acne, eczema, or something else. Many times, it first appears during the teen years; the hormonal changes of puberty can also make an existing skin problem worse. Unfortunately, not all skin conditions go away. There are some that, while not dangerous, are amazingly persistent. Often, they wax and wane, which is another way of saying they cycle back and forth between better and worse. Sometimes they go into total remission, disappearing entirely for awhile, only to make a surprise—and unwelcome—return appearance. All of this is what we mean when we say a condition is chronic.

Acknowledging that you have a chronic condition can be difficult both for you and your parents. It amounts to accepting a problem in your future that you never thought you would face. But you don't have to feel like a victim. If Kim's diagnosis turns out to be eczema, she and her mom should know that she can do lots to take control of her situation and turn her skin problem into a mere inconvenience.

Here are some of the most common chronic skin conditions that teens face.

ECZEMA

Next to acne, eczema—also called *atopic dermatitis*—is probably the most common chronic skin complaint that doctors treat. In fact, it affects up to one in five children all over the world. So if you're coping with this condition, you're certainly not alone.

In teens and younger children, eczema shows up as extremely itchy, dry, red patches of skin, called *plaques,* that typically appear in the crooks of the elbows, behind the knees, and sometimes on the

Skin Facts: Did You Know?

Although specific foods can cause eczema flares in young children, they're rarely triggers for teens.

face around the eyes. It can also affect the feet, hands, ankles, wrist, and upper chest.

Scratching the plaques can make them redden, crack, crust, or weep fluid and often makes them worse. They may go away on their own or with the help of some moisturizers, but they often require medical treatment. Even then, unfortunately, the patches usually come back.

And then there is the itch. Sometimes it grows worse at night, so that falling asleep, staying asleep, or getting enough of the very deep slumber you need for adequate rest becomes difficult if not impossible. You can easily find yourself exhausted and distraught during the day. It may even be hard to stay awake at school and perform well.

And finally, there is the unpredictability. For some people, eczema becomes worse during the winter months and improves in the summer, but that isn't true for everyone. In fact, each person has his or her own set of triggers—things in the environment, including dust mites, pet dander, and outdoor allergens—that can cause eczema to flare. Often, the trigger is a change in the weather.

Although science doesn't really understand all of the causes behind eczema, we do know that genetics plays a major role in its development, as well as a role in the development of seasonal allergies and asthma. Doctors call this the *atopic triad,* and if you have one of these allergic conditions, you may also have another. This does not mean that one causes the other. And it doesn't mean your parents caused your eczema or allergies, so don't blame them. These conditions are very common and becoming more so each year.

Treatment. Eczema can deeply affect your life in many ways. First of all, the appearance of plaques can deliver a blow to your self-esteem, making you feel embarrassed about the way you look and less than enthusiastic about going out in public. But that's not all. A person who has been up all night scratching an itchy rash will end up exhausted by the time school starts the next morning, so academic performance often suffers as well. Obviously, managing this condition is an important priority in the life of any teen who has to cope with it.

Keep in mind that the most important consideration for any chronic condition, even before treatment begins, is to find a doctor who will be your ally and work with you over time—especially as your feelings change about how you want to treat your skin and as new products come onto the market.

Treatment involves a four-pronged approach:

▸ Moisturizing
▸ Reducing inflammation
▸ Controlling infection
▸ Reducing itch, primarily at night

Moisturizing. Dryness is a part of having eczema, and keeping your skin moist is critical. An old-school idea for doing this was simply to bathe less, but nowadays doctors recommend taking a brief—no longer than 10 minute—bath or shower every day. Staying in the water any longer may temporarily relieve the itch, making you feel better, but ultimately you'll end up feeling worse because it will dry your skin. Use a fragrance-free soap (chemicals that smell nice can also irritate your skin) with a pH of 7, such as Dove Sensitive Skin (bar) or Cetaphil Gentle Cleanser (liquid). Also, wash with lukewarm water. Hot water dries the skin.

When you dry off, pat with the towel, and don't rub. Any scratching will worsen your symptoms and the rash itself.

After your bath or shower, moisturize immediately. If the doctor has prescribed a topical medication for you, apply it first, then spread your moisturizer over top of it. Some doctors may want you to apply your moisturizers at a different time of the day. If it's convenient for you, that approach is okay too. Good moisturizing creams come in tubes and jars. Lotions, on the other hand, dispense from a pump and don't contain enough oil to be effective for very dry skin. There are plenty of great products to choose from—Cetaphil, Eucerin, CeraVe, and Vanicream, to name just a few. Thicker products such as Vaseline or Aquaphor give great results, but they're generally better for use at night when you don't have to worry about looking greasy. Avoid fragranced bath products. Also, avoid perfumes or colognes on your skin. (An occasional dab of perfume on your clothing, however, won't worsen your eczema.)

Reducing inflammation. Treating the redness (inflammation) with medications such as topical corticosteroids and a new class of drugs called topical calcineurin inhibitors is the mainstay of therapy for eczema.

Topical corticosteroids come in strengths of low, medium, high, and superpotent. The strongest drugs are usually reserved for use on the hands and feet where the skin is thicker. For the more delicate skin on the face, low-strength corticosteroids and calcineurin inhibitors such as Protopic ointment or Elidel cream are more appropriate. Whatever you use, it is important that you feel comfortable with the way it feels. If your doctor prescribes a greasy ointment that you're never going to use, you need to speak up and say so. There are effective, nongreasy options in each strength group.

Low-potency drugs are also more appropriate for other areas where the skin is thin, such as your groin, the crooks of your elbows, and the backs of your knees. However, in these areas, it is okay to use higher potencies for a few days at a time to get symptoms under control.

Like all medications, these drugs have potential side effects, but those side effects are easy to manage—especially since your doctor will be monitoring you. Don't be afraid of using these medicines. They will give you relief and heal your skin. Just don't skip your regular doctor's appointments.

Treating Infection. People tend to scratch their plaques so vigorously that infection often develops within the areas of eczema. The bacteria most frequently involved in this situation is *Staphylococcus aureus,* commonly known as staph. More rarely, a drug-resistant strain of this germ, called *methicillin resistant Staphylococcus aureus* (MRSA), can cause problems. By no means are these life-threatening diseases, but they are a nuisance because they often make the dermatitis worse. They can also be difficult for a patient to recognize. So here is what to look for: If you're using your medication as you're supposed to for several weeks and you're still not getting better, it's time to call your doctor. You either have an infection, the medications are too weak, or you're not using the medications effectively. He or she will be better able to determine how to proceed. If it turns out that you do have an infection, you'll probably need to take an oral antibiotic. Your doctor may even suggest that you add bleach to your bathwater a few times a week. This can really help treat an infection and prevent it from coming back.

Reducing Itch. Getting enough rest is important both for your health and your life in general. If you're itching so badly that you

When to See a Doctor

A rash is an extremely common finding in many illnesses, some of which are serious, but most of which, fortunately, are not. So how do you know when it's time to see your doctor? If you have a persistent rash that doesn't go away over a couple of weeks, especially if it's accompanied by fever, weight loss, aches and pains, or muscle weakness, call your primary-care physician and make an appointment. You should also see your doctor if you are worried about skin infection.

can't sleep, then an antihistamine that both reduces the irritation and makes you drowsy, such as diphenhydramine (Benadryl) or hydroxyzine (Atarax), may help. For daytime itching, you can try nondrowsy antihistamines. They're not effective for everyone, but it certainly wouldn't hurt to give them a try.

Support. People with obvious and visible chronic skin problems often suffer from embarrassment and low self-esteem. The first step in coping with these emotional challenges is to find a community of support. People with eczema often seek support and help from the National Eczema Association. Find out more at www.nationaleczema. org.

KERATOSIS PILARIS

These are the fine, flesh colored or red bumps—actually plugged follicles—that appear on the backs of the arms, sides of the cheeks, front of the thighs, and sometimes the buttocks. Although they don't hurt or itch, they can make your skin feel like sandpaper to the touch. If you have this condition, you inherited it from either your mom or your dad or perhaps both of them (it's very common). Like a chronic illness, it waxes and wanes over time, but it is not a true disease. In fact, it is simply a skin type that is prone to plugged follicles. You can treat it with moisturizers that contain keratolytics such as glycolic acid, alpha glycolic acid, lactic acid, or urea, as well as some prescription medications, but you need to apply these products regularly to keep it smooth. Unfortunately, this is the skin that you have been given, but in many people find it improves as they get older. Ask your parents—they may have outgrown it.

ICHTHYOSIS

This is actually a group of inherited, chronic conditions of extreme dry skin. The most common, called *ichthyosis vulgaris,* affects one in every 250 people. It occurs when the normal shedding cycle slows down and dead cells build up on the surface of your skin. The telltale sign is the formation of tiny plates of dead skin that look like fish scales, primarily on the front of the lower extremities. Sometimes, however, they can appear all over the body. In addition, you may notice deep and prominent lines on your palms and soles. Many but not all people who develop ichthyosis also have eczema, and the two conditions seem to be connected.

Treatment. Regular short baths or showers; lukewarm water; fragrance-free, pH-balanced soap; and regular moisturizing are the keys to successful treatment. It's a lifelong condition, and if one parent in a family has it, his or her children all have a 50 percent chance of developing it as well.

PSORIASIS

Psoriasis affects 2 to 3 percent of the population, and for many kids, it will make its debut during their teen years. It generally appears as red, scaly plaques that are most prominent on the elbows, knees, scalp, and sites of friction or trauma, but it can appear anywhere on the body.

Skin Facts: Did You Know?

The word *ichthyosis* comes from the Greek word *ichthys*, meaning "fish." The condition is so named because it can make human skin look like scaly fish skin.

When it happens to a teenager, psoriasis often first will appear as multiple, smaller, teardrop-shaped spots all over the body instead of the larger areas we see with adults. This is called guttate psoriasis. It may also first appear in the groin or on the genitals, and it can make your nails ridged and brittle.

Unlike eczema, psoriasis is not usually itchy, but it is often difficult to clear completely. It can wax and wane, sometimes disappearing completely, only to come roaring back in a flare-up. Unfortunately, although the skin lesions can go away, they never really go away forever. It is a lifelong condition.

We believe that psoriasis is an autoimmune condition, meaning it is a symptom of the body mistakenly attacking its own healthy tissue. During one of the steps of this process, immune cells in your skin chemically signal other cells to overproduce. That's what causes the plaques and scaling. The immune cells also cause inflammation.

Doctors don't completely understand why all of this happens, but we strongly suspect that for you to develop psoriasis, you must have a genetic predisposition toward the disease—that is, some of your genes are not behaving properly. Often, a psoriasis patient will have a parent or grandparent who also coped with the condition or a similar one. A trigger—some unusual event or exposure—also seems to set the stage for the disease to appear. For example, sometimes psoriasis will first emerge after a strep throat, so we know that the infection has

Psoriatic Arthritis

Although very rare, a teen who has psoriasis may also begin to feel pain, stiffness, and swelling in his or her joints. This may signal the appearance of a joint-skin disease (also an autoimmune condition) called psoriatic arthritis. Joint problems often begin in the fingers or hands, although they can also start in one large joint such as the knee. There is no cure, and treatment often includes the use of anti-inflammatory medications, immune system–inhibiting drugs, pain relievers, physical exercise, and rest. Symptoms may also occur the other way around: A teen may develop the arthritis of psoriasis first and later experience a skin flare.

acted as a trigger. Stressful life events can also cause cause psoriasis to flare for some teens and adults.

Treatment. To treat this condition, you may have to use topical medications such as corticosteroids, retinoids, vitamin D3 cream, coal tar liquid, or for severe cases, systemic drugs—either injectable or oral. Some of these systemic medications slow down skin cell production. Others, called *biologics,* interfere with your immune response.

Psoriasis often improves in the summer because UV radiation actually helps control it. In fact, having psoriasis is one of the only circumstances in which a physician will ever tell you that it's good to get a controlled amount of sunlight, "just a little tan." An experienced dermatologist may even use light therapy, utilizing specialized ultraviolet lamps, to help bring your psoriasis under control. This does *not* mean, however, that you should start a do-it-yourself program at a tanning salon. Stay away from those places!

Psoriatic nail changes are very difficult to treat. You will either need injections of corticosteroid into your cuticle area (a very painful choice) or systemic (oral or injectable) treatment. There are more potentially serious side effects with systemic treatment, so doctors use it only in the most severe cases. The scalp is generally treated with medicated oils, foams, and shampoos.

Support. The National Psoriasis Foundation offers a great array of support groups, both online and face-to-face. Find out more at http://support.psoriasis.org.

VITILIGO

This is a condition in which the pigment, melanin, completely disappears from areas of the skin. Like psoriasis, it may be due to an autoimmune reaction. Some experts believe it occurs when your pigment cells, called melanocytes, attack and destroy themselves.

The most common areas affected include the ankles, knees, wrists, fingers, around the eyes, and mouth, but vitiligo can also occur as a generalized condition that affects large areas on the body. If the eyebrow, eyelash, or scalp area is involved, white hair can develop there. You can use hair dye to hide these changes in the scalp if you feel the need. Many teens with this problem develop halo nevi, that is, moles surrounded by a white ring. This means that over time—usually anywhere from many months to years—the mole is slowly going to disappear.

Many parents want to know what blood tests can be done to determine what is causing the problem and how to fix it. This is not a result of dietary or vitamin deficiencies. Like the other problems in the chapter, the cause is unknown, and it runs in families. The only time a blood test is really necessary is when there is a history of auto-immune conditions, such as certain thyroid problems, in the family, but that is rarely the case.

Treatment. Unfortunately, once vitiligo occurs, there is treatment but no cure. Medications, usually a combination of topical corticosteroids and topical calcineurin inhibitors (Protopic Ointment and Elidel Cream, usually used for eczema) can sometimes help reverse the process and bring the pigment back, but unfortunately, this result is usually partial and may be temporary. Different forms of light treatment can also improve pigmentation in some people.

There are lines of makeup that can help conceal the white spots. Covermark and Dermablend are two brands to try that are available at pharmacies and on the Internet.

Support. For a lightly pigmented person this condition may seem like a minor nuisance, but it can be devastating for an African-American, Asian, or dark-skinned individual who develops it on the face. If you feel vitiligo is making a serious, negative impact in your life, it is

Magical Cures from the Internet

Chronic skin conditions can be frustrating and depressing, no doubt about it. Because of that, it's very tempting to look for magical cures—and the Web offers buckets full of them. Unfortunately, where these diseases are concerned, the Internet is like a garage sale: Most of what you find is junk. Certainly, taking safe supplements or changing your diet is very unlikely to give you the cure you're looking for (although it might make you feel healthier). Every once in a while you may stumble across a treasure, but the odds are that your doctor already knows about these exceptional finds if they're worth anything and will be glad to talk to you about them. The bottom line: The online world is great for finding a lot of things, but miracle cures aren't among them.

very important that you get social and emotional support. One great place to start is National Vitiligo Foundation at www.nvfi.org.

HYPERHIDROSIS

Excessive sweating of the palms and soles is a common problem for kids, and unfortunately, it typically worsens with puberty. No one really knows why it happens, but it can really drive you crazy. For some people, it becomes so severe that dripping moisture makes writing difficult and certain athletic activities, such as balancing on a balance beam or holding onto parallel bars, nearly impossible. It can also make you slip out of your shoes or cause you to avoid shaking and holding hands.

Treatment. Although you can't really cure this condition, there is a lot you can do to manage it. Always start with the mildest, simplest treatment, then progress to stronger ones, if necessary. The simpler ones have fewer side effects and are safer for your body.

Drying agents constitute the first line of defense. One is an over-the-counter product called Certain Dri, 12 percent–aluminum chloride preparation and can be applied every night or every other night to your underarms, palms, and soles. If this doesn't work to your satisfaction, the next step would be to use a stronger (20 percent–aluminum chloride) prescription medication called Drysol. This can be applied nightly if you can tolerate it, but it can cause red, dry irritated skin. Twice-weekly application may be enough to control the nuisance sweating.

If you're still not happy with the results, you can proceed to oral systemic medications that block a chemical in your body called acetylcholine. This chemical transmits signals from the nervous system that tell your body to sweat. One common medication of this type (anticholinergic) is called Robinul (glycopyrrolate). It might give you side effects of dry mouth and constipation, but the dose can be adjusted to help your symptoms, and you don't have to take it all of the time. You take it temporarily for a special event such your prom or a gymnastics competition, and then stop use. The annoying side effects might just be worth a break from sweating.

Some teens will take the next step and have *Botox* (dilute botulism toxin) injected into their palms, soles, and underarms to decrease sweating. This works, but it is an expensive and painful procedure, and insurance usually doesn't cover it. Finally, there are surgical treatments for hyperhidrosis, but most dermatologists don't recommend them, as they can have significant, permanent side effects.

An Alternative Therapy for Excessive Sweating

One treatment for your hands and feet that may be effective when prescription-strength antiperspirants don't work is called *iontophoresis*. The process is simple: A device sends a mild electric current through a pan of water in which you immerses your extremities. You'll need to do this every other day for five to 10 days, then go on a maintenance schedule of one to four treatments a month. This process definitely works for some people, but no one knows exactly how or why. If you're interested in giving it a try, talk to your doctor. The iontophoresis units can be purchased on the Internet.

Support. You can learn more about this condition from the International Hyperhidrosis Society Web site at www.sweathelp.org.

WHAT YOU NEED TO KNOW

▸ Chronic skin conditions wax and wane but often persist for years, and many will last a lifetime.

▸ Eczema is a common disease of red plaques that can be treated by moisturizing, reducing inflammation, controlling infection, and reducing itch. It is very important to use your medications regularly and follow your doctor's directions. It will pay off in less itch and better sleep.

▸ Keratosis pilaris is not really a disease, but rather a type of skin that tends to develop blocked pores and form tiny, sandpaper-like areas of rough skin.

▸ Ichthyosis is a lifelong condition of dry skin that can be treated with moisturizers and good gentle bathing habits.

▸ Psoriasis is a lifelong condition that usually shows up in teens as teardrop-shaped plaques of inflamed, scaly skin. It generally doesn't itch. It is treated with topical medications, and less commonly, systemic drugs and UV light.

▸ Vitiligo is the depigmentation of areas of skin. In teens with dark skin, the effects can be emotionally devastating. Treatment can be somewhat successful, and effective covering makeup is available.

▶ Excessive sweating can usually be helped with antiperspirants at either over-the-counter or prescription strength, depending upon which is appropriately effective. For extreme cases, anticholinergic pills can be used.

▶ Many chronic diseases can be emotionally difficult for teens who have them. Finding a community of support is important.

7

Are You Contagious?

Mike sits in the waiting room of his doctor's office, trying to read an old copy of *Sports Illustrated* magazine to take his mind off the scaly rash that suddenly appeared on his forearm a couple of days earlier. He's a little nervous—he has no idea what it is.

Another patient walks in and looks around for a seat. She's a young woman, in her early twenties, with hives on her face and neck. The guy sitting three chairs away looks up. For the past 10 minutes, he has been scratching his arms and sides hard enough to wear a hole in his shirt.

How do these people make you feel? Would you prefer that the young woman sit next to you? If that guy with the itch offered you a handshake, would you want to take it? The idea of coming into closer contact with these folks might not seem so appealing.

So why is that? You don't know them. They have never done you any harm. One word: *contagious*. Whatever they have, you don't want. And just as important, you don't want to pass whatever you have to them either. You don't yet know if anyone in the room is actually contagious, of course, but something in you gets a little queasy about the idea of sitting near them.

In fact, the majority of skin conditions are not communicable. For the most part, you don't really need to worry about contracting a serious illness just because you gave someone with a rash an affectionate hug. But it does make some sense to know which conditions can pass from one person to another, both for your own good health and for the protection of those around you—especially the people you care about.

THE FOUR CONTAGIONS

Infections happen when foreign organisms first invade and colonize your body, and then begin damaging tissue or cells. Not all infectious organisms go from person to person, but most that do will fall into one of these four categories:

> ➤ Fungal
> ➤ Bacterial
> ➤ Viral
> ➤ Parasitic

Other skin conditions, such as acne, allergic dermatitis (poison ivy rash, nickel dermatitis, etc.), autoimmune disease (psoriasis, vitiligo, etc.), and cancer are not contagious and cannot be spread from person to person.

FUNGAL INFECTIONS

Fungi, which include yeast, molds, smuts (fungal parasites that feed on vegetation), mushrooms, and toadstools, are a sort of plant, but they don't contain any chlorophyll, the chemical that gives vegetation its green color and allows it turn sunlight into energy. Instead, they feed on organic matter to get their fuel. If that organic matter is you, you have an infection.

Various types of fungus make their homes on distinct areas of the body: Tinea capitis is the *scalp ringworm* (the term *ringworm* is a misnomer—no worm is involved); tinea corporis (ringworm of the body) sets up shop on the body; tinea cruris gives you *jock itch*; and tinea pedis is the culprit behind *athlete's foot*. All are contagious. You can pick up a fungus infection from skin-to-skin contact with someone who has it, touching a fungus-contaminated object or surface, or touching an infected animal.

Wrestlers and athletes in similar sports are particularly vulnerable to these infections. If you practice a close-contact sport and you have active fungal lesions on your skin, you need either to keep them completely covered or take a break from the sport until they have completely cleared away.

All four types of fungal infections are very similar, but for treatment purposes, doctors divide them into two groups: those that occur on the face and scalp and those that occur from the neck down. This division is based on how it will be treated. Lesions on the face and scalp almost always need to be treated with oral medicines.

Occasionally, a very small fungal infection on the face can be cured with a cream alone.

From the neck up. If you have an itchy, scaly scalp and dandruff shampoos or other over-the-counter products don't help, you may have scalp ringworm. Other signs include scaly skin-colored or red patches that may expand or drain fluid, pus bumps (scalp pimples), abscesses or large soft areas of swelling with fluid drainage, patches of hair loss, or scalp tenderness. If you show any of these symptoms or know that you have had exposure to a fungus through a person, object, or animal, you need to see a physician to get a *culture* done. A culture is a simple, painless test that can determine if you have fungus growing on you, and if you do, what kind of fungus it is. A scalp culture involves taking a skin scraping or swab; sometimes it involves removing a few hairs.

The only consistently effective treatment for scalp or face ringworm is prescription antifungal medication, either *griseofulvin,* terbinafine, fluconazole, or itraconazole taken orally. Often these are used in combination with an antifungal shampoo or cream. Therapy can last anywhere from four to 12 weeks. When you're finished, if all goes well and you take your medicine correctly, you should be completely cured.

Many pediatricians still treat scalp ringworm with a cream alone. That may relieve it temporarily but will never cure it. The cream is most helpful in treating the spread of smaller lesions that can occur on your neck and shoulders.

From the neck down. Ringworm of the body often causes a few circular (ringlike) red, scaly spots that appear on the trunk, neck, or extremities. Jock itch shows up as a scaly, itchy rash over the groin, inner thighs, and/or buttocks. Athlete's foot appears as red, crack-

Skin Facts: Did You Know?

You should *never* treat a fungus with topical cortisone. It will temporarily improve the rash, but it actually drives the fungus deeper into the skin, making the infection more difficult to cure with topical creams alone.

ing, peeling skin that itches and may also burn and sting. It can also blister. Athlete's foot is most often found between the toes (for some reason, the fungus really likes that space between your fourth and fifth toes). All of these infections are treatable with topical over-the-counter medications such as terbinafine, *clotrimazole,* or *miconazole,* and others and are usually applied twice a day, sometimes for several weeks. If these products don't work, you can certainly talk with your doctor about using a different topical or oral prescription product.

BACTERIAL INFECTIONS: IMPETIGO

Bacteria are microscopic single-celled organisms that come primarily in three shapes: rods, spheres (cocci), and spirals. They reproduce by dividing in two. Some are harmless to humans, but many create toxins that can cause severe health problems. Only a few target the skin.

The most common bacterial skin infection doctors see is impetigo. This is a localized, contagious condition, involving either staph (*Staphylococcus aureus*) or strep (Group A streptococci) bacteria. It affects mostly small children, but people of any age can acquire it. In adults, it happens when bacteria that normally live harmlessly on the skin's surface invade a wound. The germs then produce a toxin that attacks surrounding tissue and allows them to grow and spread. You can pick up the bacteria through contact with the wounds of infected people, or rarely, by touching contaminated objects.

Symptoms can include red scaly crusted sores, scaly blisters, and rarely, deep ulcers. You need to check with your doctor to determine how best to treat this infection. For very mild cases, keeping the wound clean and applying an over-the-counter antibiotic ointment may be all you'll need to do. More commonly, however, a prescription-strength topical antibiotic will give the best results. If the infection is severe or spread over a large area, an oral antibiotic such as cephalexin may be the treatment of choice.

If the impetigo is caused by methicillin-resistant *Staphylococcus aureus* (MRSA), a strain of bacteria that has become resistant to many antibiotics, your doctor will prescribe an antibiotic used specifically to treat that microorganism.

VIRAL INFECTIONS

Viruses are so small that they're invisible even to an ordinary light microscope. However, you can see them with special electron microscopes. A virus infects by entering a host cell and replicating itself. Like bacteria, many viruses are harmless. Unfortunately, many are not. Below are the three that most frequently cause problems for teens.

Herpes simplex virus (HSV). Herpes simplex virus (HSV) comes in two varieties: HSV 1, or oral herpes, and HSV 2, or genital herpes.

Most people are exposed to oral herpes during childhood or their teen years when they come into contact with someone else who has it—and an infected person can transmit the virus even when he or she has no symptoms. The initial infection may cause a fever, small blisters or sores in the lip or mouth area, and even a sore throat that can be mistaken for strep. Or it may cause no symptoms at all. Once the virus has established a home in your body, it never leaves. As a result, one-quarter to one-third of everyone with oral herpes will reactivate the virus intermittently, and many of these people will experience recurrent *fever blisters* or *cold sores*—actually two names for the same thing.

Recurrent active infection often begins with a tingling, itching, or painful sensation (called the *prodrome*) somewhere on or around the mouth. Shortly afterward, a blistering, sometimes crusted sore develops on the site. Generally, these lesions will heal without scarring. Several triggers can start a recurrence. These can include recent illness, intense sun exposure, or trauma to the area of infection.

Prescription antiviral medication, either *acyclovir,* valacyclovir, or famciclovir, taken by mouth at the first sign of an outbreak can shorten the length of each cold sore episode, but if you have more than six episodes a year, consider going on a preventive daily treat-

Aphthous Ulcers

If a lesion occurs on your lips or outside of your mouth, it's likely to be a cold sore. If it's on the inside, however, it's probably a canker sore, medically known as an aphthous ulcer. Canker sores are painful white ulcers that occur on the soft tissues inside the mouth. They are not contagious and will normally go away on their own in a week or so. Ibuprofen will give you some relief. If you have a canker sore that seems unusually large or that doesn't heal, have your doctor or dentist examine it. Rarely, these lesions can be a sign of a more serious condition.

ment. This prevention routine usually goes on for six to twelve months at a time.

There are many topical treatments available that don't offer the proven effectiveness of the oral treatment, but there is really no harm in trying them. The best and most effective treatment is one of the prescription antiviral medications for each episode or for prevention. Using Vaseline, Aquaphor, or some other emollient over the affected area can help a cold sore heal more quickly.

If you're prone to cold sores, try to avoid extreme sunlight. Wear sunscreen, hats, and don't go out during peak hours of UV radiation (10 A.M. to 3 P.M. in the summer and an hour later in the winter).

If you suspect you have genital herpes, characterized by small red bumps or blisters on or around the genitals, burning sensation in that area, or any discharge, you need to be examined and evaluated by your doctor during an episode.

Chickenpox. Most people have already had chickenpox—a once-in-a-lifetime event—when they were young children. A few, however, don't acquire the disease until they're older. It is caused by the varicella virus, which, like many other viruses, can make a permanent home in you and reappear later in life. In young kids, chickenpox is usually a mild illness, characterized by fever and a bodywide, itchy, blistering rash that can last for a couple of weeks. When teens and adults have it, however, they tend to get sicker.

For anyone over 13, treatment of varicella will probably include taking acyclovir or some similar antiviral—the same drugs used for herpes. You can treat the symptoms with cool baths and pain relievers, but *never* take aspirin while you have this disease. It has caused some people, particularly children, to develop a secondary disease called Reyes syndrome, which can be very dangerous and even deadly. Although chickenpox occurs only once, the virus can cause another, often very painful, condition called shingles to appear later, usually in older adults. There is now a vaccine given routinely to all children that can either prevent a chickenpox breakout or lessen its severity if it develops.

Molluscum contagiosum. These tiny, shiny, pimplelike lesions, usually pink or flesh-colored with a central depression (doctors call it umbilication), are extremely common and can last anywhere from a couple of months to a couple of years. They are caused by a pox virus, affect only the skin, and are completely harmless. The virus spreads through skin-to-skin contact, so like fungal infections, they're more common among contact-sport athletes, such as wrestlers, and they tend to appear on areas of skin where the contact occurred. Some kids develop only one or two lesions during their lifetime, but some will get a hundred of them, and others, despite exposure, will never get any. This condition is rare in adults because most people develop immunity as young children or teenagers.

Molluscum contagiosum lesions will eventually go away on their own. They can be treated with freezing therapy or a blistering agent called cantharone (the juice of the blister beetle), or by mechanical removal called *curettage*. None of these are home remedies. A pediatrician, family doctor, or dermatologist needs to do the treatment.

Verruca vulgaris. This is a fancy name for common warts caused by the human papillomavirus (HPV). There are over 100 different types, including those that cause flat warts, which we often see on the face, others that make plantar warts on the feet, still others that prefer the hands, and other types that appear in the genital area.

Most warts are harmless, but some varieties that show up on or around the genitals and the anus can cause cancer in both men and women. If you have warts in these areas of your body, you should see your doctor for evaluation and treatment (if you are a girl, consider seeing a gynecologist).

A wart can last for a couple of years or many more, but if you're patient enough, sooner or later it will go away on its own. On the other hand, if you want to be proactive and speed up the process, you can treat common nongenital warts at home with salicylic acid plasters or liquids, both available at most pharmacies. These remedies

HPV Vaccine

HPV is behind most of the cervical cancer that women develop. To help stop this disease, the FDA recently approved a vaccine that is extremely effective in preventing the two most prevalent types (70 percent) of cervical cancer and the two most common types (90 percent) of genital warts. The vaccine is delivered through three injections over time in a doctor's office. If you feel it may be appropriate for you, talk with your parents and your doctor about it.

Skin Facts: Did You Know?

Liquid nitrogen, sometimes used to freeze unwanted lesions such as warts off of skin, is a cool −320° F, cold enough to liquefy the air around it.

will work better if you cover the wart and medication with a self-adhesive bandage or duct tape. Typically, after an application you'll wait for a day or two—until the tape comes off—then pare away the dead skin and reapply the plaster or liquid. It can take months of treatment to get the result you want, but even so, it will still be faster than doing nothing.

For the fastest results, you can go to a dermatologist for treatment. Generally, his or her first choice will be to freeze the wart with liquid nitrogen. This is done to kill the skin that the wart virus is living in. This approach is painful, often causes a blister in the treated area, but will most likely not leave a scar.

Yet another option your doctor can offer is *immunotherapy*. With this method, an allergen is painted on your skin to induce an allergic reaction. As your immune system kicks into high gear, it also attacks the wart virus.

There are a few treatments available that are less likely to help and may actually do more harm than good:

> ▶ **Surgery.** Generally, dermatologists don't like to remove warts surgically, as the procedure leaves a scar and there is a high likelihood (up to 50 percent) that the wart will grow back.
> ▶ **Cimetidine.** In theory, a heartburn medication called Tagamet (cimetidine) works like immunotherapy—by stimulating the immune system to attack your warts. Research on the drug, however, has shown mixed to poor results for this use.
> ▶ **Home freezing.** Home-freezing kits contain coolants that are applied to the wart to kill the skin the virus is living in. However, they aren't nearly as cold as the liquid nitrogen used by doctors and often don't achieve the deep skin freeze that's necessary. They might be worth a try for early warts that are less thick.

> **Cantharone.** This is the juice of the blister beetle. When it's used to remove warts, the lesion will sometimes grow back in the shape of a ring (a "ring-wart").
> **Lasers.** Although lasers have been used successfully to remove warts, they're really no more effective than other destructive techniques like liquid nitrogen or surgery, and they're many times more expensive.

Finally, there are probably more folk remedies for wart removal than for any other skin condition. They include rubbing on everything from garlic paste to aloe gel. People swear by them, and some may actually work. Almost anything that causes irritation will bring on an inflammatory response from the immune system, and that may be enough in some cases to make the wart go away. Most of these remedies are at least harmless. As long as you know a remedy won't hurt you, give it a try!

PARASITIC INFECTIONS

Parasites are organisms that invade a host organism—in this case, you—feed off of it and do it harm. The major parasites that attack the skin are bugs—insects and arachnids such as *scabies* and the various forms of lice.

Lice. It's hard even to hear the word without feeling the creepy crawlies all over, and almost nothing will cause school administrators to panic more quickly than a student who comes to school with an

Scarlet Fever

If you develop an diffuse itchy, fine, bumpy red rash (a "sandpaper rash"), that is more prominent in your groin and the folds of your underarms and elbows, ask your doctor to check your throat! It may well be a symptom of a strep infection that has traditionally been called scarlet fever. With this infection, you're contagious until you have been on antibiotics for two days.

infestation. Lice, however, are a fact of life. They can infest anyone who is unfortunate enough to become exposed. It does, however, take close personal contact to transmit them. Lice crawl from person to person. They don't hop or fly. Pets and wild animals, by the way, don't carry these pests. That distinction belongs to humans alone.

Lice come in three varieties: *body, head,* and *pubic lice (crabs).* Body lice (*Pediculus humanus corporis*) are the only lice that transmit disease, particularly typhus. They live in clothing and only make contact with the skin when they feed on blood. Generally, a diagnosis of the condition is made by examining the seams of clothing for crawling lice and nits (eggs). Although poor hygiene and crowded living conditions certainly play a role in your risk for acquiring them, they can happen to anyone who is exposed. That means close personal contact with an infected person, clothing, or other personal belongings (including mattresses, sofas, etc.).

Head lice (*Pediculus humanus capitis*) live on the head and neck and they lay their eggs at the base of hair shafts. They're the most common type of lice in the United States. Generally, a younger child will acquire them from another child, then pass them along to the family. Personal hygiene has nothing to do with your risk for getting this infestation. It happens when an infected person's hair (or comb, brush, pillow, carpet, etc.) comes into contact with the hair of an uninfected person. Although they are fairly common among other ethnic groups, they are rare among African Americans.

Pubic lice (*Pthirus pubis*), also called "crabs" because their shape, generally live in the pubic area but can appear on other parts of the body and head, including the eyebrows and eyelashes. They appear among all ethnic groups and all social classes. The most frequent way they're transmitted is through sexual contact, but like the other two types of lice, they can also be transmitted through clothing, bedding, etc.

For body lice, regular bathing and clothes laundering are the only treatments necessary. For head lice and pubic lice, prescription medications are available, but over-the-counter remedies are extremely effective. These items contain either *permethrin,* pyrethrins, and/or *piperonyl butoxide,* all of which are safe and effective against these pests. Follow the instructions on the package. Don't use these chemicals around your eyes. If you find crabs or nits in your eyebrows or eyelashes, you can remove them with a fingernail or you can get a prescription treatment from your doctor. Don't use a cream rinse or conditioner just before applying medication to your scalp. For head lice, you'll need to remove the nits with a special comb after applying the medication. If you discover any more crabs nine or 10 days after treatment, re-treat.

Skin Facts: Did You Know?

Head lice nits need to stay close to a warm human scalp to maintain a constant temperature. If one falls off, it will die within a week.

For body lice, again, good personal hygiene will do the trick. For all lice, make sure that the personal belongings of all infected persons are thoroughly cleaned or discarded. Clothing should be washed at a temperature of 130°F or higher, and they should be dried in high heat twice. Alternatively, you can store belongings in plastic bags for two weeks, which will prevent the parasites from finding new hosts and allow them to die. Obviously, you should not use any personal items belonging to an infected person that have not been sanitized. By the way, it isn't necessary—and may be harmful to people and pets—to spray with insecticides or fogs to get rid of these infestations in your home. Finally, if you have pubic lice, you should contact any person with whom you have had sexual activity over the past month and let them know.

SCABIES

Scabies are microscopic mites that burrow into the upper layers of human skin, where they make themselves at home and lay their eggs. The mites are contagious. They pass from one person to another through prolonged skin-to-skin contact, such as during sexual activity. An infected person can transmit the mites even though he or she may not yet be having any symptoms, which generally don't appear for the first two to six weeks.

The most common symptoms of scabies infection are itching and a pimply red skin rash. This rash most often appears between the fingers, on the wrists or ankles, under the arms, in the genital area, or around nipples. The itching, however, does not come from their saliva. It occurs when your body develops an allergic reaction to the mite and to the feces they leave in your skin. Sometimes, their burrows are visible on the skin. They look like raised, crooked or flesh colored lines.

There are no over-the-counter medications you can use to rid yourself of these little parasites. A doctor will need to prescribe a *scabicide*, that is, a drug especially formulated to kill scabies mites and their eggs. You apply the medication topically, usually spreading it over your entire body from the neck down. Generally, if one family member is known to be infected, the entire family will receive treatment at the same time.

The itching can persist for two to four weeks after the scabies mites and their eggs are all dead, as it results from an allergic reaction, not from direction action of the living mites. Your doctor may follow you closely during this time to make certain another treatment isn't necessary.

Any clothing, bed linens and blankets, towels, or washcloths the infected person has used three days prior to treatment should be washed in hot water and dried in a hot drier or else sealed in a plastic bag for 72 hours. The mites will generally die within three days if they can't find a human host to live in.

WHAT YOU NEED TO KNOW

> - There are four main types of contagion: fungal, bacterial, viral, and parasitic.
> - The four common sites of fungal infection include the scalp, body, groin area, and feet. A doctor must treat scalp ringworm with oral medication. Anything below the neck can usually be treated with over-the-counter topical medication.
> - Impetigo is a bacterial infection involving either staph aureus or strep organisms. Treatment is topical for most cases, oral for severe or widespread cases.
> - Herpes simplex comes in two forms—oral and genital. Its most characteristic symptoms are blistering sores. It often goes dormant after the initial infection, then recurs. Genital herpes should be evaluated by your primary doctor, or if you are female, a gynecologist.
> - Molluscum contagiosum is a contagious viral infection that appears as skin-colored or red, pimplelike lesions with a central depression. It is extremely common and considered a normal childhood infection. It will go away on its own.
> - Verruca vulgaris, also called warts, are caused by the human papillomavirus (HPV). There are over 100 types. The mainstays of treatment are removal by freezing or other destructive methods. Home remedies like salicylic acid pads or liquid may

be helpful. Genital warts need evaluation by a primary doctor or gynecologist.

➤ Lice are parasitic arthropods. Three types affect humans: head lice, body lice, and pubic lice. Good personal hygiene and laundering will cure body lice. Over-the-counter medications, along with nit removal, are excellent treatment options for head and pubic lice.

➤ Scabies mites are nearly microscopic, parasitic red mites that infect the skin. You'll need a prescription scabicide to get rid of them.

8

Your Hair and You

Jeff is worried. Something is happening to his hair. When he showers in the morning, thick clumps of it block the drain. The bristles of his brush have become tangled with it. And he swears he can see white scalp peeking through what was once a thick, black mane. The problem is that he is only 17, and he is really afraid that he's going bald. In fact, he has become so obsessed with examining his scalp and hairline that he can't walk past a mirror without checking it from every possible angle. He, of course, wouldn't call it an obsession—just a reasonable concern. After all, his dad is pretty thin on top, as was his grandfather, and Jeff vaguely knows that hair loss is hereditary.

His mom, always a comfort, has tried to convince him that baldness passes down through the mother, and all of the men on her side of the family grow hair as thick as mink fur. Unfortunately, he isn't buying it. Of all the catastrophes that can happen to a young person, this seems to be the worst, and he is sure it is happening to him. He tried fishing for reassurance from his girlfriend, Stephanie, but she turned out to be remarkably unhelpful. Apparently, she isn't very attracted to bald guys. And there it is—the gist of it for Jeff: He believes no one is attracted to bald guys. He is convinced that he'll never have another girlfriend, and he'll become the butt of jokes among his friends. He will ultimately end up alone, miserable, and looking 20 years older than his actual age.

For Jeff, there is only one pertinent question regarding his situation: What can he do to stop it?

129

WHAT IS HAIR?

Your scalp is an amazing organ. It can maintain a crop of 80,000 to 100,000 strands of hair, and you don't have to do a single thing to cultivate it. That crop keeps you from losing body heat and acts as a shock absorber for the top of your head. Each strand starts in a bulb deep in your skin, where the hair is made with an insoluble protein called keratin. As new cells push the old toward the surface, the new ones die, just as skin cells do. In the case of hair cells, however, all the keratin they carry begins to elongate and intertwine into a long, thin thread. This eventually yields a visible hair that is extremely strong, durable, and flexible.

The type and texture of your hair—straight, wavy, curly, kinky—depends upon the shape of the follicle, which in turn results from genetics. Very cylindrical follicles produce straight hair. More oval-shaped follicles that grow at a sharper angle to the surface of the scalp make curlier or kinkier hair. Hair gets it color from pigment cells (melanin) that saturate it early in its growth cycle.

When we talk about healthy hair, we don't really mean that the strands on your scalp, which aren't alive, can really have good health. What we mean is that it grows normally, and it is undamaged, with its roots in a healthy scalp.

BASIC HAIR CARE

When hair has a bad day—when it looks dull, dry, limp, or frizzy—it may simply be due to the amount of humidity in the air, or it may happen as a result of the way it has been treated or overtreated. If you

Skin Facts: Did You Know?

The human body actually grows three kinds of hair. The first, *lanugo hair*, is a soft, downy fur that covers you while you're still in the womb and disappears three months before you're born. The second, vellus hairs, are the short, colorless, "peach fuzz" hairs that grow everywhere but your palms, soles, and lips. The longer colored hairs that grow on your head and selected other parts of your body are called *terminal hairs*.

have damaged your hair with bleaches, processing, or overwashing, you may have given yourself brittle hair shafts and split ends. And unfortunately, once hair is damaged, it can't repair itself. Remember, it's not alive. So to avoid bad hair days, here is what to do.

Washing, conditioning. Proper hair care mostly comes down to using the right products for your hair type—normal, oily, or dry—on a regular basis. How do you know which hair type you have?

- **Normal.** If your hair holds its cut or style easily without becoming limp, flat, frizzy, knotted, or tangled, and it doesn't have breaks or split ends from previous perming, *bleaching,* or dying, choose a shampoo and conditioner designed for normal hair.
- **Oily.** If your hair tends to be limp, flat, or thin, making it difficult to style, and feels "oily" to the touch, it may be holding a little too much sebum from the follicle. Choose a shampoo and a special conditioner designed for oily or greasy hair. If you have very fine hair, you may also benefit from using these products.
- **Dry.** If your hair feels dry, frizzy, knotted, and/or tangled, has split ends, or has been damaged by perms, dyes, or bleaches, choose a mild shampoo specially formulated for dry hair. Many conditioners are designed to help with this problem.

When you actually wash your hair, don't twist, twirl, or scrub it vigorously, and don't push it into piles on top of your head. Those are all good ways to create tangles and knots. Instead, wet your hair with lukewarm water, put some shampoo into your palm, apply it to the scalp, and work it out toward the ends of the hair with a gentle massaging motion. One shampoo application will do. Two—especially if you have dry hair—may be overdoing it. Different conditioners are designed to be applied in different ways, so follow the bottle instructions carefully, especially with regard to how long you leave it in your hair.

When drying, first pat most of the moisture out of your hair with a towel, and then do a gentle combing to remove any tangles. If you want to use a hair dryer, now is the time. Keep the setting low and as cool as possible. A powerful blast of hot wind can damage your locks.

Dyeing and bleaching. Whether or not to change your hair color is, of course, a very personal decision, but it is not one that you have

Green Hair

Have you ever gone for a dip in a chlorinated pool and come out with green hair? Surprisingly, it's really not the chlorine itself that gives you that color. The green comes from metals that are present in the water. Fortunately, there is an easy fix. You simply need to use a specially formulated chelating (metal-removing) shampoo. There are several available that you can purchase online. Some people use lemon juice or vinegar, but commercial shampoos work best. This is mostly a problem for swimmers.

to make in one step. Dyes come in various forms—temporary, natural, semi-permanent, and permanent. Temporary and natural dyes wash out after just a few shampoos, so if you end up with a color you don't like, you won't have to live with it forever. Semi-permanent dyes last for eight to twelve weeks, giving you a chance to live with a color for awhile and decide if it's a good match for the long term.

Permanent dyes last until your hair grows out. Preparing the hair to accept them requires bleaching—a process whereby you actually take the color out of the melanin in your hair through a chemical process called oxidation. Once that change has occurred, you can't reverse it, so be sure you have the color you want before you go permanent. Bleaching can also make the hair brittle and dull, so once you've done it, you may need to use specialized conditioners to get the look you want. By the way, hair that is overbleached will turn yellow—the natural color of the keratin. It is wise to have a professional hair stylist do permanent color changes to your hair, rather than trying to do it yourself.

Finally, some people have had allergic reactions to permanent dyes, especially one containing a chemical called *ammonium persulphate*. Always ask your stylist to do a small test patch before applying a dye all over your scalp.

Perming and Straightening. Permanently setting waves or curls into your hair by perming, or alternatively, using chemicals to straighten your hair make alterations to the molecular bonds that hold your hair's keratin strands together. These alterations are permanent unless you change them with even more chemicals. So a perm really is permanent—at least until the hair grows out. And to keep it looking good, you'll have to repeat the perming process every month as new hair grows. We have all seen tresses that have been worked and reworked with these processes until they look lusterless and brittle. So consider the possible results carefully before deciding to have your hair repeatedly permed or straightened.

HAIR PROBLEMS

Hair problems are more often about self-esteem than medical consequences, but that doesn't mean they're not important. Like Jeff's situation with hair loss, anything that negatively affects the appearance of your "crowning glory" can seem like the end of the world—not just because of the way you look, but also because it sets you off as being different from other people your age, and not in a way you like.

The hair problems that doctors see mostly fall into three general categories: scalp inflammation, hair loss, and excess hair.

SCALP INFLAMMATION: DANDRUFF

Healthy hair begins with a healthy scalp. We have already discussed scalp problems, both infectious, such as ringworm and lice (see chapter 7), and autoimmune/allergic reactions, such eczema and psoriasis

Prematurely Gray Hair

Scientists used to believe that hair turned gray because the scalp was no longer able to produce enough melanin to color new strands. More recent research, however, has shown that hair cells produce hydrogen peroxide, a natural bleaching agent that bleaches the hair gray. Another chemical, called catalase, breaks down the hydrogen peroxide in the hair of most young people before it can do any damage, but because of a genetic trait, some individuals lose the ability to make catalase at an early age. The result is a build-up of hydrogen peroxide that leads to premature graying. For teens with premature graying who feel embarrassed about it, dying may be a good option.

(see chapter 6). There is one scalp problem, however, that we haven't yet looked at: dandruff, also known as seborrheic dermatitis, doesn't happen only to your scalp. It can also affect your ears, eyebrows, and the lines that run from your nostrils to the corners of your mouth (nasolabial folds).

Dandruff is an inflammatory condition that you can sometimes improve just by using moisturizing products, but on the scalp it often requires a dandruff shampoo for mild cases and a prescription shampoo, foam or lotion, in more severe situations. If you notice flakes in your hair or on your collar, start by using an over-the-counter shampoo that contains selenium sulfide, tar, zinc, or salicylic acid. Any of these active ingredients will help remove the scales from your skin. There are also a few hydrocortisone 1 percent products you can purchase over the counter that may help reduce the underlying inflammation. But if none of these shampoos give you the results you want, talk with your doctor about using a prescription-strength product.

HAIR LOSS

No one wants to lose his or her hair. Unfortunately, for some teens, *alopecia,* as it's medically known, is a fact of life. Generally, it happens in one of two patterns: Either the hair thins out over broad areas of the scalp, or it falls out in patches. Knowing the loss pattern will give your doctor a clue as to what is causing it and what, if anything, you can do to slow it down, stop, or reverse it. Here are the common conditions that cause teens to lose their hair.

Alopecia areata. With this condition, the hair usually falls out in patches. No one is sure exactly what causes the problem, but doctors suspect that something triggers the immune system to mistake normal body tissue—in this case, hair follicles—for foreign organisms. The resulting autoimmune attack on the follicles causes hair loss.

Alopecia areata is fairly common. Two percent of U.S. population—5 million people—have it, and your chance of developing it is 1.7 percent over your lifetime. It often first appears during childhood or adolescence, usually with one or more discrete patches of smooth baldness on the scalp. There are however, two other types of alopecia areata: alopecia totalis, which causes all of the scalp hair to fall out, and alopecia universalis, which causes all the hair on the entire body to fall out. With all of them, the lost hair often returns spontaneously after a few months, or, sometimes, years.

When a patient first sees a physician about alopecia areata, he or she is often told that the hair loss is caused by stress. It isn't. Stress is part of everyone's life, but it is not the cause of alopecia areata. While it is true that stress may represent a small piece of the puzzle, and for some individuals, it may trigger a recurrence, treating stress will not make the condition go away.

The goal of treatment is to stimulate hair to grow back more quickly than it would on its own. Steroid injections into affected sites, potent topical steroids, and topical immunotherapy—applying a chemical that causes an allergic rash—can stimulate hair to grow in some people. Doctors sometimes also suggest trying topical minoxidil, an over-the-counter medication known to restore some hair growth in people with other types of hair loss.

People who have less than 50 percent hair loss respond better to treatment than those who have more extensive loss. If you have totalis or universalis, treatment success is low, but your hair may still come and go on its own. Unfortunately, the cycle is unpredictable.

Those who lose their eyelashes may need to use an eye wash frequently, as dust particles will get into your eyes more easily.

Dealing with severe alopecia areata can be frustrating and depressing, and treatment options aren't great. But it is something that millions of others have learned to live with successfully, and with time, support, and a few learned coping skills, so can you.

Begin with your appearance. If losing scalp hair bothers you, it may be time to look into finding an attractive wig or other hair prosthesis to cover the bald area. You might also talk to your teachers or school administrators about the possibility of wearing a hat or scarf in class.

It's often helpful if the school nurse, your mom or dad, or a teacher talks to your class to explain the condition and reassure your classmates that you do not have cancer and it is not contagious.

Finally, a word about the Internet. There is no lack of people in the world who will try to make a profit—whether in dollars or strokes to their ego—from your misfortune. Don't fall for them. If you go online

Skin Facts: Did You Know?

Princess Caroline of Monaco, daughter of Grace Kelly and Prince Rainier, has alopecia areata.

looking for a cure, you will find hundreds of "cures," and it's very likely that none will work. It's an invitation to heartbreak.

Rather than wasting your precious time and money on worthless remedies, you might find it worthwhile to focus more on learning how to live with this condition. Working with a counselor or therapist can help, and becoming involved with the National Alopecia Areata Foundation (www.alopeciaareata.com or www.naaf.org) is generally a very good idea.

Androgenetic (or androgenic) alopecia. Many people call it male pattern baldness, but it affects both men and women, and unfortunately, it may be what is causing our friend Jeff to lose his hair. It is a type of genetic hair loss.

Normal hair growth happens in a cycle with three phases:

> **Anagen.** This is the growing phase of the cycle. It usually lasts between two and six years and determines to what length your hair can grow.
> **Catagen.** This is a transitional stage, during which the hair follicle rests and prepares for shedding.
> **Telogen.** This is the shedding phase of the cycle, when your hair comes out naturally. We can normally lose more than 100 hairs per day as a result of this part of the cycle.

A hormone called DHT (dihydrotestosterone) can significantly shorten the *anagen phase* of the cycle in people who are born with a genetic sensitivity to it. The shortened time causes hairs to miniaturize more with each cycle, until they're finally more like "vellus hair" (peach fuzz) than terminal hairs.

Androgenetic balding can start in the teen and even in preteen years. Males typically thin at the crown and hairline. For women, the hair loss tends to happen more evenly over the top of the head, but

Skin Facts: Did You Know?

The idea that male pattern baldness is passed down only from mother to child is a myth. The gene can come from either parent.

the hairline doesn't move back. Women may also notice a widening of the part.

The most common treatment for teens is topical, over-the-counter medication, minoxidil, which comes in 2 percent and 5 percent strengths. Although the lower strength is marketed toward women and the higher strength toward men, either sex can use either one safely and effectively. The 5% solution is more irritating to the scalp, as it contains more alcohol, but it is now available in a foam which lessens that side effect. The only other significant side effect with topical use is hair growth in areas where you don't want it, such as your cheeks and forehead. To avoid that, simply keep the medication off of your face and apply as directed. Minoxidil only works for as long as you use it and takes up to six months to improve the thickness of miniaturized hairs. If you stop applying it, your hair loss will start again.

The only other treatment approved by the Federal Drug Administration for the treatment of androgenetic alopecia is an oral medication called finasteride, which is also used for conditions of the prostate gland. Males under the age of 18 and any female who might become pregnant can not use finasteride. It has significant side effects and can cause birth defects.

Surgical treatments, such as transplants, seem to help some people, but many don't find the results desirable or natural looking. There are also a wide variety of hair pieces for men and women in all price ranges.

A young person who is going bald in this way can easily find him or herself depressed or panicked in the short run, and can lose confidence and self-esteem in the long run. Women may have an especially difficult time adapting to their situation, as much of our culture's idea of female beauty involves a beautiful mane of hair.

Learning to accept yourself as you are is extremely important in coping with this condition. If you feel you need counseling to help you get through it, don't be shy about finding someone who can be sympathetic to your feelings and give you the support you're looking for.

The greatest fear that people have when facing a permanent, unwanted change in their appearance is that they will be teased, or at the least that no one will be attracted to them. If you're losing your hair, it is true, some people won't be attracted to you. The same would be true if you were taller, shorter, thinner, fatter, darker, lighter, richer, or poorer than you are. But many people—perhaps most— won't really care what your hair looks like. They'll see nothing but your beautiful eyes, or killer smile, or nice hands, or great physique.

Or how about your irresistible laugh, sparkling conversation, kind heart, unbeatable courage, or quick wit? Aren't the people that see these other qualities in you more worth your attention?

Telogen effluvium. Diffuse hair thinning that happens after a serious illness or trauma such as a severe flu, high fevers, or surgery, is called telogen effluvium. It usually occurs several months after the event. No one knows why it happens, but don't worry, your hair will thicken again on its own.

This is probably the most common type of hair loss we see among teens. If you suddenly notice that your ponytail looks smaller, there is more hair on your hairbrush or pillow, or that you're leaving more behind in the shower, talk to your parents and doctor about it. They may be able to help you pinpoint the cause—some physical stress that occurred over the past six months.

It's probably also a good idea to make certain you're getting enough iron and protein in your diet, as anemia can contribute to this kind of hair loss. That would be rare, as anemia is likely to give you other symptoms long before you start losing hair, but it's always a good idea to cover all bases.

Certain medications can also have this effect, so go over your list of medications with your doctor.

Traction alopecia. This type of hair loss is a result of tension and pulling on the hair, often caused by tight ponytails and braids. It is most common among African-American girls. It tends to occur at the outermost margin of the hair where it's pulled tightly. Often, pustules will appear in the area, or just thinning at the margins of braids or the frontal hairline. The hair loss can be permanent, and scarring can occur if the braids aren't loosened. Some people seem to be more prone to traction alopecia, even when other family members are not.

Trichotillomania. This is a habit of pulling, twirling, plucking, or rubbing your hair that breaks the shafts and causes temporary hair thinning and bald patches. Trichotillomania can affect your scalp hair or your eyelashes and eyebrows. Most people who have one of these habits aren't aware of what they're doing. A person might twirl a front lock or rub an eyebrow as he or she falls asleep, reads, writes, or watches TV. He or she might have other obsessive tendencies, as well, such as nail biting, acne picking, or even thumb sucking. Usually, these inclinations improve with time and a little help from distraction techniques.

When to Call the Doctor

Hair loss is rarely a cause for medical concern. However, some conditions do need to be under a doctor's care. Any hair loss on the scalp that is leaving scars, draining fluid, or swelling is a sign to call your dermatologist or primary-care physician.

If the problem persists throughout your teen years, however, and you find giving it up too difficult, you should not be embarrassed to seek help from a psychiatrist who has experience with teens and obsessive behavior. Although it can be difficult for kids—and even their parents—to admit there may be a problem, without that admission, it is very difficult for a doctor to help you.

HAIR REMOVAL

Not everyone with a hair problem is concerned with losing hair. Some people—especially young women—have excess hair, and usually in places where they don't want it, such as the chin, upper lip, legs, and arms.

There are many ways to remove hair, some more permanent than others. Here are some to think about:

Laser hair removal. This is the most popular way to permanently remove hair from anywhere on your body. It can be quite expensive, but as it has grown more popular over the past few years, more and more laser centers are offering package deals that can significantly lower the cost. If hair removal is very important to you, you might think about asking for one of the packages as a Christmas or birthday present.

There are many types of lasers available for hair removal, so be sure to have a discussion with your chosen laser center to make certain you'll have access to the most up-to-date technology. You will have to receive multiple treatments to get the results you want, and even after you've finished, you may have to return from time to time for touch-ups. Light hair is more difficult to remove with lasers than dark hair. That's because dark hair absorbs the laser light better than light hair does.

Laser hair removal can be painful, but anesthetic pain creams are available, and if you have a low pain threshold, it is certainly worth asking for the cream. Also, taking ibuprofen prior to the procedure can help reduce discomfort.

Electrolysis. This technique uses a very fine needle—thinner than a human hair—to enter hair follicles and deliver a mild electric current. Although it may sound painful, because the needle is so small and doesn't actually break the skin, there is only minimal pain—if any—involved. Some people do feel discomfort from the electric shock. The downside of this approach is that it can take up to two years of return visits to make the hair removal permanent.

Creams. Creams basically come in two varieties: bleaching creams and depilatories. Either can be purchased at your local pharmacy or over the Internet. Both are inexpensive, but neither can remove hair permanently.

Bleaching creams take all of the color out of hair by a chemical process called oxidation. These creams don't make the hair go away, but they do help to make it less noticeable. Most people feel no pain with this approach, but a few complain of an itching sensation afterward. Don't bleach near your eyes, mouth, nose or genitals. And don't use bleach on irritated, exfoliated, or sunburned skin. Also, never use a metal dish or metal applicator with the bleaching cream.

Depilatories contain acidic chemicals that dissolve the proteins in hair. They're available in lotions and liquids for larger areas such as your legs, and as cream for more targeted application, for example on your face. The depilatory will take anywhere from five to 15 to minutes to work after application. After you wash it off, you should find smooth skin underneath—but it doesn't work equally well for everyone. The main drawback to depilatories is that they have a distinctive, somewhat unpleasant odor while they're working.

With either a bleaching cream or depilatory, test it on a small area of skin and wait 24 hours before doing a full application. That way, if you're allergic to anything in the product, you can avoid spreading it all over yourself.

Shaving. Shaving is certainly the most common way for young men to remove unwanted facial hair, and young women often use it to remove hair from their legs and underarms. Improper shaving technique can leave you with uncomfortable irritation, razor bumps, and ingrown hairs. With that in mind, here are some tips to get a good result with your razor.

Boys and Men:

> **Wash** your face with a pH-balanced soap to take off any grime that might clog or snag the razor blade.

> **Rinse** with warm—not hot—water. This will help soften your beard. You can hold a warm, wet cloth for a minute or so to your face, which will soften the whiskers. Some men like to shave in the shower, which is okay as long as you have unbreakable, non-fogging mirror affixed in the shower stall.

> **Apply** a dollop of shaving cream with your finger tips. Use a glycerin-based cream rather than a foam—it will give you better lubrication. Do it in a circular, upward motion to help lift the hairs up from the face. Using a shaving brush (a badger-hair brush is best) with the same circular motion does an even better job. Do *not* apply a thick layer of lather. It will only clog your razor and make shaving more difficult.

> **Shave** with a multiple-bladed safety razor—*not* a cheap, disposable razor. Shave the cheeks, mustache, chin, and neck in that order. The neck comes last because it has the toughest whiskers and the most delicate skin, so it makes sense to give it a little more time to soak in the shaving cream. Make short strokes in the same direction that the hair grows, and rinse the blade off in lukewarm water often as you shave. If you feel you really must shave against the grain for a smoother result, shave with the grain first, then go in the opposite direction afterward. Do *not* rinse the blade in hot or cold water, as the temperature can change the shape of the blade and cause cuts.

> **Rinse** any excess shaving cream off of your face with cool water, then pat dry with a towel.

> **Apply** a moisturizer to keep it from drying out, itching, and burning. Do *not* use an alcohol-based aftershave or cologne.

> **Change** your blade often. Ideally, you should get rid of the old blade after three uses.

Girls and Women:

> **Trim** longer hairs down to stubble length with scissors or a hair trimmer, especially under the arms or along the bikini line, before you shave.

> **Soak** in a warm bath or take a warm shower before shaving. This will soften the skin and the hair you intend to shave.

> **Apply** shaving cream to the area you want to shave. Use a glycerin-based cream, as it will give you better lubrication.

> **Shave** with a multiple-bladed safety razor with disposable cartridges rather than a cheap, disposable razor. For your legs,

make short, gentle strokes starting from the ankles and moving upward, against the grain of the hair. For bikini line and armpits, shave in the direction of the grain. For your underarms, be careful not to shave too close—it can cause painful irritation and bleeding.

➤ **Rinse** off with cool water and pat the area dry.

➤ **Apply** a skin oil or moisturizer to your skin to help keep it soft, supple, and reduce irritation.

➤ **Change** your blade often—with every shave if you can, but no less than once every three shaves. A used blade will have nicks in it that can cause you to cut yourself.

Trimming. This is really the only way to get rid of unwanted nose and ear hair, and the trimmers are generally safe and effective. Make certain to keep the blade clean.

Tweezing. This is the most common way to remove eyebrows and eyelashes. When you tweeze, remember, hair in those areas take a long time to grow, so don't expect them to come back right away like the hair on your scalp does. Before you tweeze your brows, apply cotton balls or a washcloth soaked with warm water for about five minutes beforehand. It will make plucking easier.

Waxing. There are basically two types of waxing: hot and cold. Neither remove hair permanently. Hot waxing is usually performed

Ingrown Hairs

An ingrown hair is one that becomes embedded in the skin, usually as a result of friction, and specifically, from shaving. Usually, they're just a nuisance, but they can lead to a folliculitis, which is an inflammation around the area. Chronic ingrown hairs are sometimes treated with a topical antibiotic that also acts as an anti-inflammatory. In rare cases, ingrown hairs can lead to scarring; in such cases doctors like to be more aggressive, using topical or injectable steroids or even laser removal of hair in areas where ingrown hairs are likely to occur.

by a professional esthetician. Cold waxing can be done at home and usually come in a kit with wax and cloth applicators. Follow the product's directions closely when you use it, but be warned: This is a potentially painful procedure. Taking ibuprofen beforehand can help reduce pain. Some people are more prone toward ingrown hairs from waxing, and others from shaving, so experiment and find what works for you. If you wax your eyebrows, avoid using topical retinoid acne products there, because the skin can become more fragile in those areas.

Vaniqa. This is a new prescription product (www.vaniqa.com) that miniaturizes the hair (reduces its size) so that it is less noticeable. It is approved for use in adults, but it does have some side effects, including burning, tingling, stinging, and redness of the skin. You should tell your doctor if any acne-like pimples or any bumps occur after you use Vaniqa. Rarely, individuals have had serious allergic reactions that include rash, itching, swelling, and trouble breathing.

FINGERNAILS AND TOENAILS

Nails are there to protect the nerve-rich, sensitive ends of your fingers and toes. Normally they're smooth, but your nails can be quite funny looking—bumpy or ridged, or pitted—and sometimes this is a sign of a disorder.

Routine care includes clipping, leaving some of the white, cutting straight across, not down too deep in the corners, particularly for toenails. Biting, picking, and tearing nails and cuticles can increase your chances of infection. If you have a chronic habit of picking your cuticles or biting your nails, try to become more aware of what you're doing and stopping if you can. If you don't, your nails may actually start growing out with ridges and lines in them from all the trauma.

When getting a manicure or pedicure from a salon, make sure they autoclave their instruments. Instead of massage chairs, look for places that offer individual buckets that can be more thoroughly cleaned because bacteria are known to live in the jets of spa pedicure chairs. The technology for these chairs is improving all the time, but individual buckets are still your best bet.

Fungal infections. Fungi can infect either fingernails or toenails and can be very difficult to treat and cure. Infected nails tend to be brittle, dull, thickened, often with ragged edges. The nail may turn a dark color and even come off in worst cases. Although there are a number of over-the-counter products available, none of them cure fungal nail infection. If you suspect you have this type of infection, see your doctor for a nail culture to diagnose it. What you may think is a fungus may be something else, such as chronic trauma from running or poorly fitting shoes. If you do have a nail fungus, your doctor will prescribe one of several prescription oral medications (itraconazole, fluconazole, or terbinafine).

Hangnails. These little tags of dead skin that appear next to your fingernails and toenails can become quite painful, especially if they catch on clothing and irritate the healthy skin they're connected to. Treatment is simple. Wash the affected area with soap and water and soak it until the hangnail softens. Then, using a nail clipper or scissors that have been swabbed with alcohol, snip the dead skin off. Be careful not to cut into healthy skin, but if that happens, wash the cut, apply antibiotic ointment, and keep the wound bandaged for 24 to 48 hours.

To keep hangnails from recurring, make sure to wash your hands daily and moisturize with a thick cream, one that dispenses from a jar or tube is best (not a pump). If you bite your fingernails, work at breaking the habit. Nail biting encourages hangnails to form.

Ingrown toenails (and fingernails). An ingrown toenail can make walking and running difficult, give you constant pain, and if you don't do something about it, develop into an infection. It happens when the edge or corner of a toenail grows directly into the skin. The skin may then become irritated and painful. As the skin tears, bacteria have a way to get in and grow.

Some people develop this problem over and over again, probably because they have inherited an abnormal toenail shape or position. Occasionally, the condition results from an injury—a stubbed toe, for example. Most often, however, improper trimming or poorly fitting shoes causes the condition.

The first rule in caring for your toenails is to cut them straight across, not in a curved shape. The second is to leave them just a little long—don't cut them down to skin. The point of both of these rules is to keep the corner of the nail above the skin, not in a position where the surrounding flesh can fold over it,

If you already have the beginnings of an ingrown toenail or you know you have a tendency to develop them, after every bath or shower, loosen the edges of the nail so it doesn't continue to curl under. If it looks red, or if yellow or green fluid seeps out of it, see your doctor. He or she may prescribe an antibiotic, either an ointment or oral.

Skin Facts: Did You Know?

Any infection around the margins of a fingernail or toenail is called a paronychia. This infection can be caused by a bacteria, or sometimes, a yeast.

Ingrown nails that keep coming back should be seen by a foot specialist, called a podiatrist, who can surgically remove part or all of the nail to provide you relief. In some severe cases, the podiatrist may recommend that you have the root of the nail, the matrix, removed as well, which will prevent the nail from ever growing back.

A similar infection can occur in the folds of skin around of your fingernails. At the first sign of redness or tenderness, apply topical antibiotic ointment and clean the area several times daily with an antibacterial soap. If you see yellow or green pus building up under the skin, or the flesh around the nail remains red over several days, see your doctor. Pus is an indication of bacterial infection and may need to be drained.

WHAT YOU NEED TO KNOW

▶ Hair is composed of dead cells pushing up from a hair follicle.
▶ Choose hair-care products based on your hair type, the relative dryness/oiliness.
▶ Bleaching actually takes the color out of your hair and chemically alters its structure.
▶ Premature graying is a result of hydrogen peroxide building up in your hair follicles.
▶ Dandruff is an inflammatory condition that can be treated with over-the-counter shampoos for mild cases, prescription corticosteroids for advanced cases.
▶ Hair loss can be diffuse or patchy.
▶ Alopecia areata is an autoimmune condition that causes hair to fall out in patches. In the rarer cases of alopecia totalis and universalis, it may fall out completely from the scalp or entire body, respectively. It is a cyclical condition, and may not respond well to treatment.

➤ Androgenetic alopecia is caused by a male hormone, DHT, but happens in both men and women. For teens, the medical treatment is minoxidil.

➤ Telogen effluvium is hair loss that is usually due to a major physical stress, and it corrects itself.

➤ Traction alopecia is caused by tight pulling on the hair and can cause scarring if the cause is not corrected.

➤ Trichotillomania is hair loss due to unconscious or conscious manipulation of the hair. In persistent cases, consultation with a psychiatrist may help.

➤ Laser hair removal is the most popular technique for permanent removal. Electrolysis is also permanent but takes longer.

➤ Bleaching creams and depilatories can give good temporary results.

➤ Always soak and lather before shaving any part of the body. For beards, underarms, and bikini lines, shave in the direction of hair growth. For legs, shaving in the opposite direction is okay.

➤ To relieve the pain of any kind of hair removal, including laser removal and waxing, taking ibuprofen beforehand may help.

➤ Fungal nail infections need to be evaluated and treated by a doctor.

➤ A hangnail should be thoroughly washed, then clipped with sharp clippers. After that, treat it as an open wound.

➤ Ingrown toenails should be treated with soakings and moving the edges of the cuticle back.

➤ Red tender skin around nails should be cleaned with antibacterial soap and treated with topical antibiotic.

➤ Pus or persistent redness around the nail should be seen by a doctor.

9

Helping Others Cope with Skin Conditions

Jackie had not been to school in three days, and the rumors were flying. People were saying that she was sick, really sick. Someone had seen her just this morning, getting into her dad's car, and she had something awful on her face. The word *cancer* came up. So did the names of a few other diseases, like leprosy. But Jackie's best friend, Julie, knew better, and she had had enough of all of the gossip. Today, at lunchtime, three girls were going on about it in the cafeteria when one of them snidely mentioned "flesh-eating bacteria."

Julie exploded. "You don't know what you're talking about!" she said. "Jackie doesn't have leprosy, and she doesn't have cancer, and she doesn't have a "flesh-eating bacteria," whatever that is! She has an allergy, that's all! You can't catch it, and it's not going to eat her up."

The girls looked at her as if she were crazy, but she didn't hang around for more conversation. She picked up her lunch tray and headed out to her next class without a backward glance.

"Allergy," she knew, was not really the best description, but she didn't have to give these people every last detail of her friend's dermatitis. Jackie was missing school not because she was terribly ill, but because she was terribly embarrassed. She had a large, red blistering patch of skin on her face, and she couldn't bring herself to go out in public. And for her part, Julie was not about to let anyone make it worse for her friend than it already was.

After all, Julie herself had already experienced what the kids at school could do with a skin condition. For two years now, she had been waging a daily war with cystic acne, and she didn't always come out the winner. Some of her classmates made no secret of the fact that they didn't care to look at her. They made comments, hurtful ones, within easy earshot, and only one person—Jackie—had stood by her.

Now, at last, there seemed to be a positive side to having acne. Julie had two years of experience that she could use to help her friend. She had already taken the opportunity to recommend a doctor, a kids' dermatologist, whom she trusted. And it comforted her to be there for Jackie through several long phone conversations over the past couple of nights. Now that she thought about it, Julie was proud of herself. Just the evening before, she had actually had gotten Jackie to laugh!

PAY IT FORWARD

There is probably not a kid in the world who never has to cope with a skin condition, big or small, during his or her teen years. You certainly have. Perhaps you've had a blister on your heel that kept you out of a soccer game, or a flare of psoriasis that kept you from a prom. Whatever it may have been—or maybe still is—you have a unique opportunity to take your experience, and whatever kindness or understanding you may have received from someone else, and pay it forward. There are things you know—such as the importance of being patient, of expressing anxieties, of finding good medical care, or simply of what it feels like to stay up all night with a terrible itch—that could be valuable to someone else.

Just as importantly, you also have an opportunity to learn new things—about the skin condition of the person you're trying to help and about the importance of being a kind, caring, and good friend. Don't let this opportunity pass you by.

With all of this said, if you're still not sure exactly how you can give someone your support, there are a number of areas in which you can help them.

FINDING A DOCTOR

Even if someone has a good family doctor, it is never a bad idea to recommend a physician you have come to trust, particularly if he or she is a specialist who really understands teen skin conditions and has been able to develop a good rapport with you. Of course, there is no guarantee that a doctor you very much like will be equally appealing to your friend, but the odds are better.

If you don't know of a doctor you can refer your friend to, suggest he or she take a look at the Society for Pediatric Dermatology's Web site (www.pedsderm.net). It is an excellent source for finding a pediatric dermatologist.

ENCOURAGING COMMUNICATION

A person who is upset, depressed, or anxious about a physical problem needs people around with whom to share feelings. The first person on that list, of course, might be you, but you can take it a step further and encourage him or her to open up to others who are trustworthy as well, especially a responsible adult. Parents are at the top of the list. If that doesn't seem within the realm of possibility, a school counselor, a family friend, an aunt or an uncle, the leader of a church group—the community of friends and family are full of people who can help. Of course, reaching out is a very hard first step, but your friend will have a lot of support if he or she can do it.

SHARING KNOWLEDGE

If you happen to know someone who is coping with a condition similar to yours, you have a very special opportunity to share about what has worked for you and what sort of complications to look out for. If it's a chronic condition, you can reassure them that the future isn't really so bleak. In fact, it's full of hope and promise. After all, you are the living proof of it! You can also let them know what hasn't worked for you, particularly with regard to prescription, over-the-counter, and Internet treatments. The two of you can also work out a "buddy system" of mutual encouragement to help each of you follow your treatment program.

SHARING RESOURCES

Chronic conditions such as eczema, alopecia areata, and vitiligo can be a real challenge for people who are newly diagnosed, and it can be very helpful for them to find support from more people like yourself who may already be dealing with a similar situation. Sharing support groups, Web sites, and reading material can save another person a lot of time and effort and can keep them from going up a lot of blind alleys.

Incidentally, it's also important to let them know where *not* to go on the Web. Online chat rooms and support groups that aren't well moderated tend to attract people who are having difficulty resolving

For Friendship's Sake

Skin conditions that come from bacteria, viruses, fungi, allergens, genes, and accidents often need medical intervention, but there are some skin symptoms that signal a need for other kinds of intervention as well. In fact, they may be a cry for help, and you should be aware of them if they happen to anyone you know. They include track marks (small pin pricks from needles) along the inside vein of an arm, which might indicate drug abuse; cut marks on any part of the body, which might mean self-abuse or even a suicide attempt; and unexplained wounds, bruises, or burns, which could indicate physical abuse by anyone from a parent to a boyfriend. It is difficult to intervene in these situations. You may feel, for example, that you would be betraying a friend by bringing his or her track marks to the attention of a parent or teacher. But remember that as hard as it may be, in the long run, you might be saving his or her life—even if you lose someone as a friend. When you find yourself in a situation like this, no matter how unpleasant it may be, you need to act.

issues around their own conditions or are at the extreme end of the spectrum as far as their symptoms or disease are concerned. Talking with folks like these can be upsetting and anxiety-producing for someone who has been newly diagnosed, so you might want to warn your friend away from such Web sites. Well-known organizations, such as the National Eczema Association, the National Vitiligo Foundation, and the National Psoriasis Foundation, are all good choices when looking for support groups online.

REINFORCING TREATMENT

Caring for a skin condition always involves following some kind of treatment routine. Sometimes taking medicine can take real effort and dedication, and smearing on creams and ointments—well, it isn't always fun. So it's easy to forget or simply skip doses and applications, especially when your mood is low. This is a great opportunity for you to check in with your friend now and then and make sure he or she (and you, if you're still coping with your own condition) is following medical advice. You don't have to be obvious or pushy about it. Simply asking how the treatment is going, or how a particular drug is working can be enough to start a conversation.

You can help support treatment in other ways as well. For example, if you're old enough to drive, you can offer to give your friend a ride to his or her medical appointments. That has the added advantage of giving you some time together to talk.

LEARNING MORE

If the person you're trying to help has a condition that you're unfamiliar with, especially if is a debilitating one like psoriasis, learn everything you can through reading, conversation with knowledgeable people (e.g., your own doctor), and the Web. Find out about causes, symptoms, treatments, social impact, and the usual outcomes of the condition. Look for news about new medical discoveries. Read the stories of other people who have been through it. The idea is *not* for you to give medical advice or in any other way try to be a doctor. It is simply for you to better understand what your friend is going through.

In one important way, however, you can put your new knowledge to practical use. Every condition has its myths—that chocolate and fried foods cause acne, for example, or that stress causes alopecia areata. Listen for hints that your friend may be buying into these ideas, and if he or she does, waste no time in debunking them. You can save your friend a lot of heartache, frustration, self-blame, and worry by presenting the facts in the face of nonsense. Reassure your friends that they did not do anything to cause or deserve their skin problem.

COPING WITH MOOD

Worry, fear, sadness, anger, and depression are all perfectly normal reactions when a person learns they have a skin condition that can, in one way or another, alter his or her life forever. That is as true for cystic acne as it is for severe eczema. Sometimes, a teen's emotions and moods can become very powerful—so powerful that coping can be very difficult. This situation can be dangerous—even life threatening—and can lead to serious depression. Unfortunately, the depression itself can make reaching out for help very difficult. Paying attention to mood changes can be critical to your friend's welfare. If you notice any of the following in someone you know who seems to be depressed, alert a parent, school nurse, teacher, or counselor:

➤ Anger
➤ Complaints of aches and pains that don't seem to get better
➤ Difficulty thinking and concentrating
➤ Discussion of death or suicide
➤ Expressing feelings of worthlessness or guilt
➤ Increased sensitivity to rejection
➤ Irritability
➤ Loss of appetite or unusually ravenous eating
➤ Low energy and constant fatigue
➤ Outbursts of crying
➤ Sadness that doesn't seem to go away
➤ Signs of insomnia (dark circles under the eyes, constant yawning) or oversleeping
➤ Social withdrawal

LEARNING FIRST AID

Chronic conditions aren't the only skin problems you can help a friend with. Wounds, burns, and animal bites can require immediate action, and the person who sustains them isn't always in a condition

Why Does My Friend's Skin Look Yellow?

Yellow skin, or jaundice, is not a skin problem, but it can be a symptom of internal disease, often in the liver. Jaundice results from having an excess of an orange-yellow pigment called bilirubin in the body. Usually the liver processes this and the body excretes it, but when the liver isn't functioning properly, that doesn't happen. The most common cause of jaundice in teens is hepatitis A, a viral disease that is usually spread through food contaminated with fecal matter. While it can make you feel very sick, hepatitis A is rarely serious or life-threatening. However, there are other, more serious causes of jaundice, so if you notice this symptom in a friend, don't be shy about bringing it to his or her attention. And if you notice it in yourself, see a doctor.

to respond. Knowing how to recognize a serious allergic reaction is especially vital. You may save a person's life.

It's also important to be aware of any severe allergies among the people you care about. Remembering not to offer cookies with a little peanut oil in them to someone who is allergic to peanuts may also be lifesaving.

BEING SUN SENSIBLE

Do any of your friends have light skin and blue eyes? Freckles? Light or red hair? Lots of moles? Are there any who never seem to tan but always burn? Support your friends that are sensitive to the sun by planning outdoor activities either early or late in the day, when sun exposure won't be so intense. If they always have to wear protective swim shirts or hats, wear these too. You will be grateful to have less sun damage yourself. In addition, anyone who tends to get sun poisoning or severe sunburns will be grateful for your support.

You may also have a friend with a chronic condition or severe acne that requires regular use of medications. Some of these medications, such as some antibiotics, can cause skin to burn easily. So be a pal and help your friend avoid direct intense sunlight exposure during peak hours.

STAYING AWARE

It's not unusual for a young person who's developed a skin condition to be in denial about it. This can be harmful in many ways, but first among them is that it delays the process of getting needed help.

Denial may be less likely to happen with something like an acute infection or flare-up of atopic dermatitis, a condition that can draw unwanted attention from others. Kids who get stared at may find it difficult to claim there is nothing wrong. In fact, they're likely to become even more aware of having a problem that makes them different from their peers and are often hurt by the negative attention they receive.

There is however, one instance in which denial can be catastrophic: melanoma (skin cancer). It is absolutely critical that someone with the diagnosis of melanoma or a changing, suspicious mole get medical help quickly. Prompt action can mean a complete cure. Procrastination can mean a fatal outcome.

So be aware not only of lesions on your own skin, but also on the skin of your friends and family. Remember, people don't often get a rearview image of themselves, so someone can have a suspicious lesion between his or her shoulder blades and not even realize it's there.

Review the warning signs of a cancerous mole in chapter 2. And if you notice an odd-looking one on someone you know—or even on a stranger—a simple question such as "Have you had that looked at?" will be all you need to say.

WHAT YOU NEED TO KNOW

- ▶ You can turn your skin condition from a negative to a positive experience by sharing what you have learned about coping with someone in a similar predicament.
- ▶ Recommending a doctor can guide someone to medical care more quickly.
- ▶ Encouraging communication can help someone open up emotionally.
- ▶ Keeping an eye out for signs of self-mutilation and drug abuse and reporting what you've seen to a responsible adult can save a person's life.
- ▶ Doing a "buddy system" of mutual encouragement, as far as following a treatment regimen is concerned, can lead to a better medical outcome for both you and your friend.
- ▶ Learning about someone else's condition can help you understand him or her better.
- ▶ Being aware of someone's mood and encouraging him or her to get help for depression can save a life.
- ▶ Learning and using first aid can help a friend recover from a dire situation, especially a life-threatening one such as anaphylaxis.
- ▶ Not only is being sensible about sun a considerate thing to be for a friend, but it is also a good thing to be for yourself.
- ▶ Be aware of skin changes on friends and family, and especially of suspicious, changing moles. Your alertness could save a life.

10

Paying for Care

Joey felt as if a miracle had happened. After three years of living with terrible acne that had already left some pitting scars on his face, his parents had given him a fantastic sixteenth birthday present: They had taken him to see a dermatologist. He didn't know how they could possibly afford it, but somehow they had scraped the money together. He left with a prescription in his hand and a smile on his face. As for his parents, well, they had tears in their eyes. They took him directly to the nearest drugstore, where he presented his prescription to the pharmacist as if it were a winning hand of cards. Then a conversation started that made all his hopes and optimism come tumbling down.

"Have you ever filled a prescription here before, Mr. Mallory?" the pharmacist asked Joey.

"We haven't," Joey's dad replied, thinking the question was for him. "Is that important?"

"No. I thought we might already have your insurance information on file."

"We're not using insurance," Mr. Mallory said. "We'll pay in cash."

A concerned look passed over the pharmacist's face. And that prompted one to pass over Joey's as well.

"This is expensive medication," the pharmacist said. "Would you like me to calculate the price before I ring it up?

Mr. Mallory hesitated. "I guess you'd better," he said finally.

When the pharmacist recited the cost of the drug, Joey's mother spoke up for the first time. The way the words blurted out seemed to surprise her as much as everyone else. "We can't afford that!" she said.

And with that, Joey's heart sank.

THE COST OF DERMATOLOGICAL CARE

In some ways, skin problems can be among the least expensive medical problems you can have. Often, they're treatable without expensive surgical procedures or hospitalization, and a many require only an occasional visit to the doctor's office. Some (but not all) physicians are also willing to charge on a sliding scale (that is, on the basis of your parent's income), so while treatment may never be free, it can often be made affordable. Fees for psychological counseling, sometimes a concern for dermatology patients with chronic conditions, are very often set the same way. Seeking low-cost care at a community clinic or university teaching hospital may lower cost as well.

Unfortunately, as Joey found out, there is one area in which dermatological problems can become extremely expensive: medication. For many years, the cost of drugs was increasing more quickly than any other item in medical care across the nation. Fortunately, that upward spiral has now slowed considerably, but the price levels already achieved have put many of these drugs out of the reach of the average person with no insurance. Skin medications, especially those that treat acne, are particularly expensive, even when compared to other very expensive pharmaceuticals.

So then, how do you get the medications you need?

INSURANCE AND MANAGED CARE

If your parents have an insurance or managed care plan, it may pay a significant portion of your drug cost, as well as your doctor bills. However, most insurance plans have copays, which means that the patient may have to pay a set amount for the medication based on a graduated payment plan. Managed care and insurance plans may also place limits on what they will pay, using formularies (preferred drug lists), which limit which drugs the plan will pay for.

MEDICAID

Medicaid is a health insurance program for low- and no-income people. Funds for the program come from both the state and the federal governments, and each state sets its own rules for qualifying.

Likewise, each state has the option to cover or not cover prescription drugs, but all states do, in fact, offer coverage to low-income families. Not all, however, offer prescription benefits to everyone who uses the plan. You'll need to check with your local Medicaid administrator to see if you qualify.

Unfortunately, even if you can enroll in the program, not all pharmacies—or doctors and clinics, for that matter—will accept Medicaid as insurance. You may have to do some legwork to find out who you can or can not see with this type of coverage.

You'll probably have better luck starting with large university teaching hospitals and community clinics when looking for a doctor who accepts Medicaid. The doctor, in turn, may be able to steer you toward a pharmacy that accepts it.

LOWERING COSTS

If you find yourself among the very large group of people who fall into the low- to middle-income level but don't have insurance coverage, there are some ways in which you can lower the cost of drugs or even get them for free.

GENERIC DRUGS

These are drugs that are chemically identical or very similar to the brand-name versions but are generally less expensive. Unfortunately, some of the drugs prescribed for skin conditions haven't yet reached the market in generic form. That may happen as the patents for these drugs expire, but until then, your option to buy generics will be limited. Nevertheless, when your doctor writes or calls in your prescription, don't be afraid to ask him or her for a generic form of medication. The drug you need may be available at a reasonable price as a generic.

COUPONS

Nearly all pharmaceutical companies now offer discount coupons for their skin medications, and these coupons can save you a significant amount of money. Why would the drug companies do this? It's a marketing tactic to get you to at least try their products. So if they're offering, there's no reason not to accept. You can find these coupons on the companies' Web sites.

SAMPLES

For the same reason that pharmaceutical companies offer discount coupons, they also give physicians free drug samples to hand out to

Counseling Resources

Skin conditions, especially chronic ones that change your appearance or cause you discomfort, can present unique emotional challenges. While it's important to find support groups and have friends to help you through the rough spots, you may need some professional guidance. While the cost of these services can be quite high, there are several ways in which you can get this kind of help without emptying your bank account.

Company assistance programs. Many companies, particularly those that are "self-insured" (fund their own insurance program, usually through a regular insurance provider), offer their employees a number of free counseling visits to help with short-term emotional issues. To take advantage of these programs, however, you will generally have to choose from a list of therapists and counselors that the company provides.

Government programs. Many local governments, especially at the county level, provide health-care services to people who can't afford to pay for their own. These services may be free or adjusted to the patient's income level. Contact your county mental health department for more information.

Insurance or HMO. These programs will often pay for half the cost of seeing a counselor or therapist, but many having a maximum spending

their patients. It's a marketing technique used by the companies to get you started on a particular medication that they hope you'll purchase as a prescription when your sample runs out. Many doctors, however, give these samples to patients who may not be able to afford prescription drugs, and some may be willing to continue supplying you for as long as you need treatment. It costs the doctor nothing, and it costs you nothing—a win-win situation. Don't be afraid to talk to your physician about free samples when you go for your office visit.

limit. Additionally, many individual therapists no longer accept insurance, but will supply you with receipts so that you can get a partial reimbursement.

Medicaid. This is a state-federal insurance program for low-income families. For more information on whether your state's program covers the cost of a counselor and if you qualify for the program, contact your local Medicaid office.

Neighborhood clinics and drop-in centers. Many disadvantaged and low-to-middle income neighborhoods offer inexpensive or free health care services. Check your local yellow pages.

Pastoral counseling. If you are affiliated with an organized faith, your pastor or rabbi may be able to provide you with low-cost or free counseling, or refer you to someone who does pastoral counseling.

Private practitioner. Many therapists in private practice offer a sliding fee scale that can be adjusted to your family income level. However, they may ask to be paid for each session as you go.

School programs. Many school districts have school psychologists or counselors on campus to help students who are having emotional difficulty. These services are free.

Unfortunately, samples are becoming regulated in many university hospitals and may not be available at those institutions.

COMPASSIONATE USE

Some patients can't afford their treatment medications even with coupon discounts, and your doctors may not be able to get samples of the drug you need. If you're in this situation for a severe skin condition, ask your physician about applying for compassionate use. This basically means that the doctor will contact a pharmaceutical company for you and request that they give you the drugs for free. These firms are very often willing to do this, so it's certainly worth a try. Ask you primary-care doctor or dermatologist to work with you in applying for compassionate use. It is especially worth a try if you're dealing with severe, scarring acne or other serious skin conditions requiring extremely expensive biologic or other systemic treatments.

ONLINE PHARMACIES

Online pharmacies can be a good source of less expensive skin medications, but, as with everything else on the Internet, the old saying applies: "Let the buyer beware."

In particular, purchasing drugs from outside of the United States can be tricky, and in all cases, it is illegal. In the past, the government has been lenient with this practice, particularly for drugs imported from Canada, because there were few people doing it and they tended to be senior citizens. Lately, however the federal authorities have been paying more attention and cracking down on people who purchase drugs in this way.

PATIENT ASSISTANCE PRESCRIPTION PROGRAMS

Many pharmaceutical companies run patient assistance programs for people who can't afford their products. For specific drugs, you can do a (Google) search for the manufacturer's Web site. You can also check the following Web sites, all of which offer information on patient assistance prescription programs and can help you find one that fits you needs:

NeedyMeds: www.needymeds.org
Partnership for Prescription Assistance: www.pparx.org
PatientAssistance: www.patientassistance.com
RxAssist: www.rxassist.org
RxOutreach: www.rxoutreach.com

WHAT YOU NEED TO KNOW

- ▶ Often, medication is the most expensive part of treating a skin condition.
- ▶ You can get help with payment from your parents' insurance plan or managed care plan.
- ▶ For families that fall into the no- or low-income bracket, there is Medicaid insurance, which may pay for your drugs, depending upon your state's program policy.

➤ You can lower costs by buying generic drugs, asking for physician's samples, using Internet coupons from pharmaceutical manufacturers' Web sites, asking a drug company to grant you compassionate use, enrolling in a patient assistance prescription program, or buying from online pharmacies.

➤ While buying drugs from outside the United States can save you money, it is illegal and carries some risk of receiving below-standard merchandise.

➤ You can get help paying for counseling or psychotherapy through an insurance or managed care plan, company assistance program, school program, Medicaid, neighborhood clinic, government program, pastoral counselor, or a therapist in private practice.

APPENDIX

Helpful Associations and Programs for Skin Conditions

American Academy of Dermatology (AAD)
P.O. Box 4014
Schaumberg, IL 60168-4014
(847) 330-0230
(888) 462-3376
http://www.aad.org

American Burn Association
ABA Central Office—Chicago
625 North Michigan Avenue, Suite 2550
Chicago, IL 60611
(312) 642-9260
info@ameriburn.org
http://www.ameriburn.org

American Skin Association, Inc.
346 Park Avenue South, 4th Floor
New York, NY 10010
(212) 889-4858
info@americanskin.org
http://www.americanskin.org

Camp Discovery
American Academy of Dermatology
930 East Woodfield Road
Schaumburg IL 60173
(847) 330-8907 (fax)
http://www.campdiscovery.org
A summer camp for kids with skin diseases.

The Coalition of Skin Diseases
4301 Connecticut Avenue, NW, Suite 404

Washington, DC 20008-2369
(202) 243-0115
http://www.coalitionofskindiseases.org
A voluntary coalition of patient advocacy groups.

Foundation for Ichthyosis and Related Skin Types (F.I.R.S.T.)
1364 Welsh Road, G2
North Wales, PA 19454
(215) 619-0670
info@scalyskin.org
http://www.scalyskin.org

Inflammatory Skin Disease Institute (ISDI)
P.O. Box 1074
Newport News, VA 23601
(757) 223-0795
LaDonna.Williams@isdionline.org
http://www.isdionline.org

International Hyperhidrosis Society
Kellers Church Road,
Suite 6121-A
Pipersville, PA 18947
info@SweatHelp.org
http://www.sweathelp.org

iPLEDGE
(866) 495-0654
http://www.ipledgeprogram.com

National Alopecia Areata Foundation (NAAF)
14 Mitchell Boulevard
San Rafael, CA 94903-1953
(415) 472-3780
info@naaf.org
http://www.naaf.org

National Eczema Association (NEA)
4460 Redwood Highway, Suite 16D
San Rafael, CA 94903
(415) 499-3474
info@nationaleczema.org
http://www.nationaleczema.org

National Foundation for Ectodermal Dysplasias (NFED)
P.O. Box 114
Mascoutah, IL 62258
(618) 566-2020
info@nfed.org
http://www.nfed.org

National Psoriasis Foundation
6600 SW 92nd Avenue, Suite 300
Portland, OR 97223-7195
(503) 244-7404
getinfo@psoriasis.org
http://www.psoriasis.org

National Vitiligo Foundation, Inc.
P.O. Box 23226
Cincinnati, OH 45223
(513) 541-3903
info@nvfi.org
http://www.nvfi.org

Society for Pediatric Dermatology (SPD)
8365 Keystone Crossing, Suite 107
Indianapolis, IN 46240
(317) 202-0224
spd@hp-assoc.com
http://www.pedsderm.net

Sunwise Program (U.S. Environmental Protection Agency)
http://www.epa.gov/sunwise/contacts.html

Vitiligo Support International
West Coast Office:
P.O. Box 4008
Valley Village, CA 91617-0008
(818) 752-9002
East Coast Office:
808D Wiggington Road
Lynchburg, VA 24502
(818) 752-9002
info@vitiligosupport.org
http://www.vitiligosupport.org

GLOSSARY

abrasion A wearing or tearing away of the skin.

acne cyst An inflamed sac filled with fluid that lies within the skin.

acne vulgaris A condition in which skin follicles become plugged with dead cells and sebum, causing blackheads, whiteheads, pimples, cysts, and, in worst cases, scarring.

acyclovir A prescription antiviral medication approved for use with herpes simplex and varicella (chickenpox) viruses.

adapalene A topical retinoid used to treat acne.

allergic contact dermatitis A skin reaction to an allergen.

alopecia Hair loss. Often used as a shorthand for *alopecia areata.*

alopecia areata Hair loss caused by an autoimmune process. Can lead to total scalp baldness (alopecia totalis) and total body baldness (alopecia universalis). Usually cyclical, with periods of waxing and waning.

ammonium persulfate An ingredient in some hair dyes that has been known to cause allergic reactions.

anabolic steroid A hormone that promotes muscle growth.

anagen phase The growing phase of the hair growth cycle.

analgesic Medication that relieves pain.

anaphylaxis A severe, systemwide allergic reaction that causes swelling, can inhibit breathing, cause unconsciousness, and end in death in some cases.

androgen A group of male sex hormones. Also present in low levels in girls.

androgenic alopecia Hormone related hair loss. Often called "male pattern baldness," but it affects both sexes.

antibiotic A product made from mold or bacterial substances that can kill or inhibit the growth of microorganisms and cure infections.

anticholinergic drug A drug that inhibits acetylcholine, a neurotransmitter that, among other jobs, tells the body to sweat.

antigen Any substance foreign to the body that causes an immune reaction.

antivenin A substance that can counteract the toxic effects of venom from a snake or other animal or insect.

apoptosis A type of cell death in which the cell actually kills itself.

arachnid Air-breathing arthropods (bugs) that have four pairs of legs and no antennae.

arthropod An animal that has no vertebrae (back bone) or skeleton. Instead, arthropods have an exoskeleton, which is a segmented outer shell that covers and protects them. The arthropod group includes insects, arachnids, crustaceans, centipedes, etc.

asymmetry A lack of correspondence in size or shape on either side of an imaginary dividing line. In other words, when the two halves of a shape are not mirror images of each other.

athlete's foot Medically, tinea pedis. A fungus that infects human feet and toes.

atopic dermatitis An itchy allergic skin condition in the general category of eczema.

atopic triad Three conditions that often appear together: eczema, asthma, and seasonal or environmental allergies.

autoclave A device that uses high heat to sterilize surgical or medical instruments.

autoimmune disorder A condition in which the immune system attacks normal, healthy cells, mistaking them for harmful substances that have invaded the body.

avulsion The complete tearing away of an area or piece of biological tissue.

babesiosis A tickborne, malaria-like, parasitic disease that is sometimes fatal.

bacteria Single-cell microscopic organisms, usually in the shape of a sphere, tube, or spiral, that can cause infections.

basal cell carcinoma (BCC) The most common type of skin cancer. It can appear as a sore, a red patch, a shiny bump, a scarlike lesion, or a pink growth.

bedbug A blood-sucking arthropod that infests beds and attacks victims during sleep.

Bell's palsy Paralysis of a facial nerve causing loss of muscle control on one side of the face.

benzoyl peroxide An over-the-counter drug for the treatment of mild to moderate acne.

biologic A drug that interferes with the immune response.

bleaching A chemical process that removes color.

blister A pocket of fluid trapped in the upper layers of skin, usually as a result of friction or a burn.

bluebottle Another name for the Portuguese man-of-war, a tentacled sea creature actually made up of four organisms working together. Delivers a highly toxic, painful, and sometimes fatal sting.

body ringworm Medically, tinea corporis. A fungal infection on the human body, usually infecting the arms, legs, or trunk.

Botox Diluted toxin of a bacteria called *Clostridium botulinum.* The toxin affects organs of the nervous system.

box jellyfish A highly toxic jellyfish of the South Pacific. Its sting can kill within minutes. Also known as a sea wasp.

bruise Injury to skin and tissue where blood vessels leak blood into the surrounding area causing swelling, pain, and black and blue discoloration.

bull's-eye rash An expanding circular rash with a pale center that gives it the appearance of a bull's-eye on a target. Often an early sign of Lyme disease.

calcineurin inhibitor A drug that decreases the immune response.

callus Thickened, hardened skin.

cantharone Fluid of the blister beetle. Used for treating molluscum contagiosum.

capillary A tiny blood vessel.

catagen phase The resting phase of the hair growth cycle.

cataracts Clouding of the lenses in the eyes.

cephalexin An oral antibiotic used to treat bacterial skin infections.

chemical peel Removal of blemishes and the uppermost layer of the skin with a mild caustic chemical.

chemotherapy The use of chemicals to treat or control disease.

chickenpox An infection usually characterized by fever and an itchy, blistering rash.

chigger The larvae of the harvest mite. They look like tiny red spiders. They do not burrow into the skin, but do bite it, which can cause intense itching.

chronic condition Any condition that persists over a long period of time, typically waxing and waning and sometimes going into remission.

cimetidine A heartburn medication that is sometimes used to treat warts.

cinnabar A red dye used in tattoos.

clindamycin A commonly used topical antibiotic used for acne treatment.

Clostridium tetani The bacteria that cause tetanus, a disease that usually enters the body through an open wound. It can cause paralysis and death.

clotrimazole An over-the-counter topical antifungal cream.

cold sore Another name for fever blister. Blistering lesions on or near the lips caused by herpes simplex virus 1.

collagen A protein found in most connective tissue throughout the body. It is responsible for giving skin its smooth appearance.

colloidal oatmeal An extract of oats used medicinally to calm skin irritation and itch.

comedone A follicle blocked with a mixture of sebum and dead skin cells. An open comedone appears as a blackhead. A closed comedone appears as a whitehead.

compassionate use A policy by which pharmaceutical companies supply their products at no cost to patients who can't afford them.

contusion Another word for bruise or tissue injury.

corn A type of callus that forms on the feet.

corticosteroid A hormone that calms inflammation and reduces swelling. It is produced naturally by the adrenal glands, which sit atop the kidneys; it can also be manufactured artificially.

cortisone tape An adhesive tape that contains corticosteroid. It is used to help flatten lesions and scars.

culture A laboratory test used to determine the type of organism that is causing a skin infection. A sample for testing is usually scraped or swabbed from the skin.

curettage Surgical removal of a lesion by scraping with an instrument shaped like a scoop.

DDT An insecticide that proved harmful to people. It was banned in the United States in 1972. DDT stands for dichlorodiphenyltrichloroethane.

DEET An insect repellant that keeps mosquitoes and ticks away. DEET stands for N,N-Diethyl-meta-toluamide.

dengue fever A mosquito-borne viral illness that causes a rash, headaches, and joint pain.

dermabrasion A surgical process that removes the top layers of skin. This is sometimes used for acne scar treatment.

dermatologist A physician who specializes in skin conditions and diseases.

dermis The middle layer of skin, lying between the epidermis (outer layer) and subcutaneous tissue.

DNA The genetic material that carries your inherited characteristics. DNA stands for deoxyribonucleic acid.

doxycycline   An antibiotic, derived from tetracycline, that has proven effective treating acne and many infectious agents.

dysplastic nevus   An unusual mole that may resemble a melanoma.

ecchymoses   Large, flat bruises.

eczema   An intensely itchy skin condition that can appear as red plaques on any part of the body.

ehrlichiosis   A tickborne bacterial infection that kills white blood cells.

elastin   A protein in skin that makes it flexible and elastic.

encephalitis   A brain inflammation.

epidermis   The outermost layer of skin.

epinephrine   A hormone, also called adrenaline, made by the adrenal glands. It helps the body respond to stress by increasing heart rate and constricting blood vessels.

epithelium   A layer of tissue, made of cells, that lines all of the body's internal structures, organs, and cavities.

erythema migrans   The medical term for the bull's-eye rash of Lyme disease.

erythromycin   An antibiotic, similar to penicillin, used to treat acne and bacterial infections.

exfoliant   A substance that helps remove the oldest dead skin cells from the skin's outermost layer.

famciclovir   A prescription antiviral medication approved for use with herpes simplex virus.

fever blister   Another name for cold sore. Blistering lesions on or near the lips caused by herpes simplex virus 1.

first-degree burn   A heat or chemical burn injury that causes redness, swelling, and pain to the skin but minimal tissue damage.

flea   A small blood-sucking arthropod that typically infests animals but will feed on humans as a last resort.

folliculitis   The inflammation of a hair follicle.

freckle   A concentrated area of the skin pigment, melanin, usually a result of sun exposure.

freezing therapy   A therapy used to treat warts, often involving liquid nitrogen.

frostbite   Living tissue that becomes frozen.

fungus   A plantlike organism that contains no chlorophyll to transform sunlight into metabolic energy. It therefore feeds on other organisms to live.

gene   The basic biological unit of heredity.

generic drug   Copy of a brand-name drug, often costing less.

graft A transplanted section of skin.

granuloma Noncancerous growth in tissue usually caused by inflammation or a foreign object.

griseofulvin A prescription oral anti-fungal medication.

hangnail A torn piece of skin in the nailfold (cuticle) of a fingernail or toenail.

head lice A parasite that infests the hair on the human scalp.

heat rash/prickly heat/miliaria rubra Clogging of the sweat ducts due to high heat.

herpes simplex virus (HSV) A virus that comes in two forms, one (HSV 1) that affects the area around the mouth and another (HSV 2) that affects the genitals.

histamine Protein that the body releases in response to an allergen, irritation, or insect bite.

hive/urticaria Itchy red welt on the surface of the skin caused by histamine release.

hormone A powerful chemical that helps to regulate the body's activities. Hormones are manufactured in the endocrine glands.

hyperhidrosis Excess sweating of the palms, soles, and underarms.

hypertrophic scar A raised scar that does not grow beyond the boundaries of the injury that caused it.

ichthyosis vulgaris A genetic skin disorder that causes dryness and scaling.

immunotherapy A therapy that stimulates the immune system to treat disease.

impetigo A bacterial infection of the skin, usually involving staph or strep bacteria.

infection A state in which invading organisms do harm to the host's body.

inflammation Tissue pain, swelling, redness, and warmth in response to injury or irritation.

ingrown toenail The edge or free corner of a toenail that has become embedded in the surrounding skin.

integumentary system The body's system of outer protection, comprising skin, hair, nails, associated glands, and tooth enamel.

iontophoresis A therapy for reducing excessive sweating in the hands or feet by running a mild electric current through the upper layers of skin.

iPLEDGE A monitoring program to help reduce birth defects caused by isotretinoin use.

isotretinoin A powerful oral medication, derived from vitamin A, used to treat acne.

jock itch   Medically, tinea cruris. A fungal infection of the genitals and groin of the human body.

keloid   A scar that expands beyond the boundary of the original injury.

keratolytic   A topical medication that removes, loosens, or dissolves dead skin.

keratosis pilaris   A common condition, or skin type, characterized by small flesh-colored or red bumps on the cheeks and the back of the arms, caused by plugged follicles.

ketoconazole   An antifungal medication that comes in prescription oral, shampoo, and cream form.

killer bee   A cross between an African honey bee and a European honeybee, known for its aggressiveness.

Langerhans cells   Immune cells present in the skin.

lanugo hair   The hair that covers a human fetus. Usually shed about three months before birth.

larva   The form a baby insect has when it first hatches from its egg. The larval form generally looks nothing like the adult form.

laser therapy   The use of highly focused light that has many uses including improving the appearance of acne, removing unwanted hair, or treating red birthmarks.

lesions   An abnormal growth on or change in tissue.

lice   Tiny insect parasites that can infest human hosts. Three types affect people: body lice, head lice, and pubic lice (crabs).

Lyme disease   A tickborne inflammatory disease that causes a rash and joint, heart, and brain/nerve disease.

lymph nodes   Small, bean-shaped glands, located throughout the body, that help filter out bacteria.

malaria   A mosquito-borne, parasitic blood disease.

melanin   The pigment that gives skin its color.

melanocyte   A cell that produces melanin.

melanoma/malignant melanoma   The most deadly form of skin cancer, characterized by melanocytes that become malignant, that is, reproduce and spread to other parts of the body.

metastasize   The spread of cancer cells from one part of the body to another beyond the original tumor site.

methicillin-resistant *Staphylococcus aureus* (MRSA)   A type of bacteria that has become resistant to many antibiotics.

miconazole   An antifungal that comes in a nonprescription topical form.

milia   Tiny white bumps that appear on the face or, less frequently, on other parts of the body.

minocycline   An antibiotic, derived from tetracycline that is effective for acne.

miscarriage   A pregnancy that ends on its own before the twentieth week.

Mohs microscopic surgery   Surgery that removes cancerous skin tissue layer by layer until microscopic examination shows no more evidence of malignant cells.

mole   An aggregation of melanocytes, the cells that create skin pigment.

molluscum contagiosum   A common, contagious skin condition that causes shiny, pimple-like bumps. Harmless and self-limiting.

MRI   Magnetic Resonance Imaging. A technology that uses magnetic waves (instead of X-rays) to give your doctor a very detailed view of the inside of your body.

mucous membranes   Linings that cover all surfaces inside of your body that come into contact with air, such as the mouth and nose cavities.

nasal labial folds   The facial lines that run from the sides of the nose to the corners of the mouth.

nausea   A feeling of intense queasiness often accompanied by the urge to vomit.

nematocyst   A stinging, venomous cell on the tentacles of jellyfish and other similar creatures used for capturing prey.

neurotoxin   A poison or venom that attacks the nervous system.

nevus   A mole.

nickel dermatitis   An allergic contact reaction to nickel; often appears as an itchy rash.

nit   The egg of a louse.

nodulocystic acne   Severe acne that produces cysts and scarring.

noncomedogenic   Not known to cause plugged follicles, which would result in acne.

oral contraceptives   Birth control pills.

organ   A self-contained, uniquely shaped structure in or on the body that is made of epithelial, connective, and nerve tissue; has a specialized function; and works with other organs within a system.

pallor   An unnatural paleness of the skin.

papule   A small skin elevation or bump of any color.

parasite   An organism that lives on or in another organism, takes nourishment from its host, but does not kill it.

pathologist   A doctor who specializes in making diagnoses by examining tissue both grossly and under the microscope.

perioral dermatitis   Red lesions, similar to pimples, that appear around or near the mouth.

permethrin   A cream medication used to treat scabies.

petechiae   Tiny red or purple spots under the skin that are actually miniature bruises.

petrolatum   An ointment, made from petroleum, used to soften and moisturize the skin.

photosensitivity   Excessive sensitivity to sunlight, sometimes leading to easy burning.

picaridin   An alternative mosquito repellant for people who are allergic to DEET. Should not be applied directly to the skin.

pigmentation   The coloring in your skin, eyes, and hair.

pilosebaceous unit   A tiny shaft in the skin that contains a hair root, hairshaft, and sebaceous glands.

piperonyl butoxide   A medication used against lice infections.

pityriasis rosea   A pink, scaly, patchy rash of unknown cause that usually resolves itself over several weeks.

plaque   A skin elevation usually larger than 1 cm in size.

poison ivy, oak, sumac   Plants of the Rhus genus that excrete an oil that can cause allergic contact dermatitis.

Portuguese man-of-war   A tentacled sea creature actually comprising four organisms working together. Delivers a highly toxic, painful, and sometimes fatal sting. Also known as a bluebottle.

premature birth   Birth of a baby born earlier than 37 weeks after the beginning of the mother's last period.

proboscis   In mosquitoes, a long, tube-shaped mouth used for cutting into skin and extracting blood.

prodrome   A tingling, itchy, or painful sensation that precedes the appearance of a cold sore.

Propionibacterium acnes (*P. acnes*)   Bacteria that are active in acne lesions.

psoriasis   A chronic condition, probably autoimmune, characterized by scaly plaques on the scalp, elbows, knees, genitals, and other parts of the body.

psoriatic arthritis   A form of arthritis associated with psoriasis.

puberty   A time during which hormonal changes in the body make the sexual organs functional and secondary sexual characteristics, such as facial and body hair, female breast development, and voice change, take place.

pubic lice   Parasitic arthropods that bear some resemblance to crabs (hence their nickname, "crabs") and live primarily in hair around the genitals.

punch graft   A technique used to improve the appearance of "ice pick"-type acne scars. The scar is removed with a tool that makes a small, even, round wound, which is then filled with a small graft of the patient's own skin.

pustule   A blister filled with pus.

pyrethrins   Compounds used as insecticides to treat lice infections.

rabies   A potentially deadly viral infection, usually carried by infected animals, that attacks the nervous system and brain.

radiation therapy   The use of various types of radiation to destroy tumor tissue.

resistant bacteria   Bacteria that have evolved and can survive some antibiotic therapy.

retinoids   A family of compounds, related to vitamin A, sometimes used in the treatment of acne.

rheumatoid arthritis   A chronic, progressive, disabling disease, probably autoimmune, that deforms and causes pain in the joints and can affect other organs as well.

Rhus dermatitis   A blistering allergic rash caused by the oil of the poison ivy, poison oak, and poison sumac plants.

ring wart   A wart that grows back in the shape of a ring after treatment with liquid nitrogen or cantharone.

Rocky Mountain spotted fever   A severe tick-borne bacterial illness that causes fever, nausea, vomiting, headache, rash, abdominal pain, and joint pain, sometimes resulting in long-term or permanent health problems.

runner's toe   A nail that turns black from bleeding in the nail bed. Generally results from repeated trauma.

salicylic acid pads   Medicated pads used for treating warts or calluses.

sand flea   A tiny crustacean, shrimplike in appearance, that attacks the skin and feeds on blood.

scabicide   A medication used to eliminate a scabies infestation.

scabies   A contagious, itchy skin infection caused by mites that burrow into the skin.

scalp ringworm   Medically, tinea capitis. A fungal infection of the human scalp.

scar   Pink, brown, white, or skin-colored tissue that forms over a wound or surgical site.

scarlet fever   The rash associated with strep infection, which is typically accompanied by a high fever.

scorpion   A venomous arachnid with a stinging tail. Varieties in the United States are generally not deadly.

seabather's eruption   A papular rash that occurs upon contact with the larvae of the thimble jellyfish.

sebaceous   Literally, "greasy" or "oily." In dermatology, this term usually refers to oil-producing follicles in the skin.

sebum   The oily secretion produced by sebaceous follicles.

second-degree burn   A burn in which the outer skin later (epidermis) is burned through and the second layer (dermis) has been scorched. May require medical help, depending upon location and severity.

silicone sheet   Pieces of silicone used to reduce or prevent keloid and hypertrophic scarring.

skin   The largest organ in the integumentary system. It has three layers: the epidermis (outermost), the dermis (middle), and subcutaneous (innermost) layer.

skin flap   A piece of abraded skin that remains attached on one side.

squamous cell carcinoma (SCC)   The second most prevalent type of UV-associated skin cancer in this country; extremely rare among teens. Lesions generally appear as crusted or scaly papules, a growing tumor, or a sore that won't heal. This type of cancer can spread to other parts of the body.

Staphylococcus aureus   A harmful type of bacteria that can infect wounds.

Streptococcus pyogenes   A type of bacteria that live on the skin.

subungual hematoma   Bleeding under a nail.

sun poisoning/polymorphous light eruption   An allergic-like reaction to sunlight exposure, resulting in a rash, often papular (bumps) or urticarial (hives).

swimmer's itch   An itchy rash caused by parasites that live in permanent bodies of water, both fresh and marine. It is not contagious.

tazarotene   A topical retinoid, sold as cream or gel, that is sometimes used to treat acne or psoriasis.

telogen effluvium   Temporary hair loss, usually occurring months after a physical stress such as a severe illness. Requires no medical treatment.

telogen phase   The shedding phase of the hair growth cycle.

teratogenicity   Capable of producing birth defects.

terbinafine hydrochloride   An antifungal that comes in prescription oral form and nonprescription topical form.

terminal hair   Long, thick pigmented hair that grows on the scalp, underarms, beard and elsewhere on the body.

testosterone   A potent male hormone responsible for male secondary sexual characteristics such as body hair and low voice.

tetanus   A dangerous infection of the central nervous system, caused by bacteria that enter through open wounds.

tetracycline   An antibiotic used for treatment of acne and other microorganisms.

third-degree burn   A burn that has penetrated through all layers of skin to the tissue beneath. May or may not be painful. Always requires immediate medical attention.

tick   A blood-sucking arachnid that carries many dangerous diseases, including Lyme disease and Rocky Mountain spotted fever. Feeds on the blood of people and animals.

tissue filler   Any substance that is injected into the skin to improve appearance of wrinkles or scars.

traction alopecia   Temporary hair loss due to pulling and tension on the hair, often a result of tight braids and ponytails. Eliminating the cause will eliminate the hair loss.

trauma   Any physical damage to the body.

tretinoin   A topical retinoid used in the treatment of acne. May cause dry skin and irritation.

trichotilomania   Hair loss due to habitual twirling, rubbing, pulling, or plucking the hair. Eliminating the habit will eliminate the hair loss.

triglycerides   The chemical form that fat takes in the body and the bloodstream.

tularemia   A highly infectious disease carried by rodents and transmitted to humans primarily through the bites of ticks and other bugs.

ugly duckling   A mole that stands out in shape, size, or color from neighboring moles.

umbilication   A central pit or depression in a raised skin lesion.

urushiol   An oil produced by poison ivy, oak, and sumac that causes an itchy, blistering rash.

UVA   A type of ultraviolet radiation that causes aging and skin cancer.

UV alert   A notice from the Environmental Protection Agency that the ultraviolet radiation on a particular day is expected to be unusually high.

UVB   A type of ultraviolet radiation that causes sunburns and skin cancer.

UV index   The Environmental Protection Agency's daily forecast of the risk of overexposure to UV radiation.

valacyclovir   A prescription antiviral medication approved for herpes simplex virus infection.

varicella   The virus that causes chickenpox and shingles.

vellus hair   Tiny colorless hairs that grow all over the body ("peach fuzz").

verruca vulgaris   The common wart. Caused by various strains of the human papillomavirus (HPV), which specialize in infecting particular areas of the body. Genital warts should be evaluated by a gynecologist or urologist.

vesicle   A small blister.

virus   A submicroscopic infectious agent that invades cells in order to replicate.

vitiligo   Loss of pigmentation either in segments or over large areas of the body.

yellow fever   An often lethal viral infection transmitted by mosquitoes.

READ MORE ABOUT IT

BOOKS

American Medical Association. *American Medical Association Handbook of First Aid and Emergency Care.* New York: Random House Reference, 2009.

Barrow, Mary Mills, and John F. Barrow. *Sun Protection for Life: Your Guide to a Lifetime of Healthy & Beautiful Skin.* Oakland, Calif.: New Harbinger Publications, 2005.

Beale, Lucy, and Angela Jensen. *The Complete Idiot's Guide to Better Skin.* New York: Alpha (Penguin Group), 2004.

Day, Doris J. *100 Questions & Answers about Acne.* Sudbury, Mass.: Jones and Bartlett, 2004.

Donovan, Sandy. *Stay Clear!: What You Should Know about Skin Care.* Minneapolis: Lerner, 2008.

Fulton, James E. *Acne RX.* Newport Beach: James E. Fulton, M.D., Ph.D., 2001.

Goodheart, Herbert P. *Acne for Dummies.* Hoboken: Wiley, 2006.

Kenet, Barney, and Patricia Lawler. *Saving Your Skin: Prevention, Early Detection, and Treatment of Melanoma and Other Skin Cancers.* 2nd ed. New York: Four Walls Eight Windows, 1998.

Lowe, Nicholas J. *Psoriasis: A Patient's Guide.* 3rd ed. New York: Informa HealthCare, 2003.

Novick, Nelson. *Skin Care for Teens.* Bloomington, Ind.: iUniverse, 2000.

Rodan, K., K. Fields, and V. Williams. *Unblemished: Stop Breakouts! Fight Acne! Transform Your Life! Reclaim Your Self-Esteem with the Proven 3-Step Program Using Over-the-Counter Medications.* New York: Atria, 2005.

Schofield, Jill R., and William A. Robinson. *What You Really Need to Know about Moles and Melanoma.* Baltimore: Johns Hopkins University Press, 2000.

Wakelin, Sarah. *The Royal Society of Medicine—Your Guide to Eczema.* London: Hodder Arnold, 2007.

York-Goldman, Dianne, and Mitchel P. Goldman. *Beauty Basics for Teens: The Complete Skin-care, Hair-care, and Nail-care Guide for Young Women.* New York: Three Rivers Press (Crown), 2001.

York-Goldman, Dianne, and Mitchel P. Goldman. *You Glow Girl! The Ultimate Health & Skin Care Guide for Teens.* St. Louis, Mo.: Quality Medical Publishing, 1999.

WEB SITES

American Academy of Dermatology. "Severe Acne: 4 Types." Acnenet. Available online. URL: http://www.skincarephysicians.com/acnenet/severeacne4types.html. Downloaded June 19, 2009.

BMJ.com. Dobson, Roger. "News Extra: Study of Doctors' Smoking Habits Shows Links to 11 Types of Cancer." Available online. URL: http://www.bmj.com/cgi/content/full/330/7486/276-e. Posted February 5, 2005.

Crowe, Karen. "Under My Skin." Fujisawa Healthcare, Inc. Available online. URL: www.undermyskin.com. Downloaded June 26, 2009.

Mayo Clinic Staff. "Mosquito bites." MayoClinic.com. Available online. URL: http://www.mayoclinic.com/health/mosquito-bites/DS01075/DSECTION = risk-factors. Posted May 10, 2008.

Mayo Clinic Staff. "Piercings: Proper Care Can Help Prevent Complications." MayoClinic.com. Available online. URL: http://www.mayoclinic.com/health/piercings/SN00049. Posted February 16, 2008.

Mayo Clinic Staff. "Tattoos: Risks and Precautions to Know First: Find Out What Risks Tattoos Pose, Ways to Protect Yourself, and What to Do If You No Longer Want the Body Art." MayoClinic.com. Available online. URL: http://www.mayoclinic.com/health/tattoos-and-piercings/MC00020. Posted February 16, 2008.

National Institute of Arthritis and Musculoskeletal and Skin Diseases. "Acne." Medline Plus. Available online. URL: http://www.nlm.nih.gov/medlineplus/acne.html. Posted March 22, 2009.

Owen, Wendy. "Quit Smoking: Smoking, Can It Harm My Skin?" A2Z of Health, Beauty, and Fitness. Available online. URL:http://health.learninginfo.org/smoking_skin.htm. Downloaded June 19, 2009.

Roche. "Accutane Medication Guide." Available online. URL: https://www.ipledgeprogram.com/Documents/Accutane%20MedGuide.pdf. Downloaded June 19, 2009.

The Acne Resources Center Online. "Information on Sebaceous Glands." Available online. URL: http://www.acne-resource.org/acne-skin-care/sebaceous-glands.html. Downloaded June 19, 2009.

U.S. Food and Drug Administration. "The iPledge Program Introductory Brochure." iPledge Program. Available online. URL: https://www.ipledgeprogram.com/Documents/Patient%20Intro%20Broch.pdf. Posted December 2, 2007.

INDEX